Landscapes of

EASTERN
PROVENCE
Côte d'Azur to the Alps

a countryside guide
Third edition

John and Pat Underwood

SUNFLOWER BOOKS

Second edition © 2016
Sunflower Books™
PO Box 36160
London SW7 3WS, UK

ISBN 978-1-85691-479-6

Viewpoint, Grand Canyon du Verdon

Important note to the reader

We have tried to ensure that the descriptions and maps in this book are error-free at press date. The book will be updated, where necessary, whenever future printings permit. It will be very helpful for us to receive your comments (sent in care of the publishers, please) for the updating of future printings.

We also rely on those who use this book — especially walkers — to take along a good supply of common sense when they explore. Conditions can change fairly rapidly, and *storm damage or bulldozing may make a route unsafe at any time*. If the route is not as we outline it here, and your way ahead is not secure, return to the point of departure. *Never attempt to complete a tour or walk under hazardous conditions!* Please read carefully the Country code on page 9 and the notes on pages 71-74, as well as the introductory comments at the beginning of each tour and walk (regarding road conditions, equipment, grade, distances and time, etc). Explore *safely*, while at the same time respecting the beauty of the countryside.

Cover photograph: Grand Canyon du Verdon
Page 1: old post office at Séranon (Car tour 4)

Photographs: John Underwood; cover: Shutterstock
Maps: Sunflower Books, based on the 1:25,000 maps of the French
  IGN (see pages 7 and 73)
A CIP catalogue record for this book is available from the British
  Library.
Printed and bound in England: Short Run Press, Exeter

☀ Contents _____

4   Landscapes of eastern Provence

Vineyards below the Montagne Ste-Victoire (Car tour 10). The perfect harmony between man and nature is the secret of the French countryside.

Preface

This two-volume *Landscapes of Provence* will plunge you into the most beautiful countryside between the Alps and the Pyrenees. Nature has prepared the canvas for these landscapes over millions of years, but man has added colour, form and texture. The straight bold strokes of lavender, vineyards, planes and poplars streak across plateaus; bridges and aqueducts arc gracefully over rivers; sturdy stone towers with whimsical wrought-iron bell-cages stipple the hilltops.

If the harmony between man and nature is the key to the beauty of this countryside, nowhere is it better conveyed than in the paintings of the Impressionists and Post-Impressionists so intimately associated with the south of France — Cézanne, Van Gogh, Monet. Almost everywhere you travel a masterpiece comes to life — an isolated farmhouse awash in fields of scarlet poppies, the limestone ribs of Ste-Victoire rising above a bib of emerald vineyards, stars burning out in a cobalt blue sky over the lamplit lanes of Arles.

This is a guide to the outdoors, written for those who prize the countryside as highly as a cathedral. We want to take you along the most beautiful roads by car and, when the opportunity presents itself, park, don walking boots, pick up the rucksack and *participate* in this land-

scape. France caters marvellously for all grades of walkers, but *precise* descriptions of tours and walks for motorists are rare. Most touring guides concentrate on history and architecture, while books for walkers often outline the famous long-distance routes (the Grandes Randonnées). But these 'GR' footpaths are sometimes very demanding and, being linear, are in any case unsuitable for motorists.

Our aim has been to describe **car tours** running from the Italian border to the Pyrenees through *many* (certainly not all!) of the most beautiful landscapes in the south of France. The **walks** chosen focus on our favourite beauty spots and are those we feel offer the greatest sense of satisfaction for the effort involved, taking into account the high temperatures and humidity during much of the year. Most of the routes are circular.

This first volume of *Landscapes of Provence* travels from the Riviera to the Alps and as far west as Aix-en-Provence, from where the second book will take you to the foothills of the Pyrenees. Use *Landscapes of the Pyrenees* to carry on to the Atlantic coast!

Bibliography

It must be stressed that this is a *countryside* guide, to be used with standard guides covering the area. We always travel with:
Michelin Red Guide: *always have the **latest** edition.* Useful for finding accommodation, and the excellent plans are *vital* for navigating in the cities unless you're using a smart phone
Michelin Green Guides: French Riviera (in English), **Alpes du Sud** (in French only), **Provence** (in English).
A **good field guide**. We rely on the Blamey/Grey-Wilson guide, *Wild Flowers of the Mediterranean,* now out of print but still available on the web.
Sunflower's **Walk & Eat around**

Nice, despite duplicating the first 10 walks in this book, is useful for those on a very short break and *relying on public transport*. It also features much more about

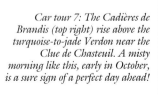

Car tour 7: The Cadières de Brandis (top right) rise above the turquoise-to-jade Verdon near the Clue de Chasteuil. A misty morning like this, early in October, is a sure sign of a perfect day ahead!

restaurants and includes recipes for local dishes.

Many French **walking guides** are available locally. Few tourist offices hand out free walk leaflets these days; they prefer to sell you a book or map. If they *do* offer a free hand-out, it is likely to be virtually useless (as we have found to our cost!).

But a real boon for walkers who read French are the online walks from the Conseil Général des Alpes-Maritimes (http://randoxygene.org). Click on 'Randonnée pédestre', choose an area, then a walk; be sure to click on 'Visualiser la carte' as well. Although the descriptions are only in French, the sketch maps are useful because they show the signpost numbers, and signposting in the Alpes Maritimes is excellent.

Note that most French publications tend to describe walks *very briefly:* make sure that you can form a mental picture of the walk in advance — ascent, distance, terrain. Read carefully what we say on page 72 under 'Waymarking, grading, safety'.

MAPS

At the top of each **car tour** we refer to the appropriate **Michelin maps** ('Local' series; scale 1:150,000-1:175,000). For this book you need only two maps, 340 (Bouches-du-Rhône, Var) and 341 (Alpes-Maritimes). For **walking** the maps in this book should suffice. But if you plan to do a lot of walking in a given area, *do* buy the relevant **IGN 'Top 25' map**. These 1:25,000 maps, published by the Institut Géographique National (the French 'OS'), are widely available in shops, petrol stations and kiosks locally, or from your usual map supplier. For each walk in this book, the IGN map number is shown.

The map **Sainte-Victoire à pied**, published by the Association des Excursionistes Provençaux, is a *must* for those exploring the mountain and surrounds (scale 1:25,000; 11th edition, 2014; 4 €). It is for sale at the Sainte-Victoire information offices in Vauvenargues and Beaurecueil, or may be ordered by email: aep.asso.aix@gmail.com.

Picnicking and eating out

Picnicking possibilities are limitless in Provence — especially if you follow the example of the locals and tour with a collapsible table and chairs (seasonally available at very low cost in many supermarkets). Picnic areas with tables are encountered on some of the tours; these are indicated in the touring notes and on the touring map with the symbol ⅋. All the walks in the book offer superb picnic settings, but on days when you are planning *only* to tour by car it is helpful to have some idea of where you might stop for an alfresco lunch. At the top of each car tour we suggest a few picnic spots, favourites of ours over the years. They are highlighted on the touring map, with a ***P*** printed in green.

It can be great fun to pick up picnic food at a local **market**. Towns and villages with markets are indicated in the car touring notes by the symbol ⅋⅋; the specific market *days* are listed in the Index.

For rainy days, or when a hot meal is called for, we also recommend on pages 174-180 some favourite **restaurants** (labelled ✕ in the touring notes). A few of these are at 'special' **hotels** where we stay regularly to break the car tours — and they vary from fairly simple B&Bs (like the Auberge at Point Sublime in the Verdon) to five-star hotels (the Pigonnet at Aix). We also explain *why* we have chosen them: sometimes it will be for the food, other-

Madone de Fenestre, with snow-capped Mt Gélas in the background — just one of the lovely picnic spots on Car tour 2

wise cooking may be a secondary consideration if they are ideal bases from which to 'watch the world go by'.

A country code for walkers and motorists

Bear in mind that all land in Provence is privately owned, whether by an individual or a district. All waymarked walks and other routes described in this book are permissive, *not* 'rights of way'. Behave responsibly, never forgetting the danger of forest fires.

■ **Do not light fires** except at purpose-built barbecues. *Never park blocking a fire-fighting track!*
■ **Do not frighten animals**. When driving, always stop the car until the livestock have moved off the road.
■ **Walk quietly** through all farms, hamlets and villages, **leaving any gates just as you find them**.
■ **Protect all wild and cultivated plants**. Don't pick wild flowers or uproot saplings. Obviously crops are someone's livelihood and should not be touched. **Never walk over cultivated land!**
■ **Take all your litter away with you**.
■ **Stay on the path**. Don't take short cuts on zigzag paths; this damages vegetation and hastens erosion, eventually destroying the main path.

☀ Touring

The ten car tours in this first volume of *Landscapes of Provence* take you north from Nice to the Alps and then west to Aix-en-Provence. While a few important centres have been omitted for lack of space, we feel that the two books present a comprehensive overview of the most beautiful landscapes. And as a change from motoring, we highly recommend the delightful train journey described on pages 168-170.

The touring notes are brief: they include little history or information readily available in guides of a more general nature. *We concentrate instead on route planning*: each tour has been devised to follow **the most beautiful roads** in the relevant region and to take you to the starting point of some delightful **walks**. (Further information about some of the places visited can be found in the notes for the walks.)

The double-sided fold-out map is designed to give you a quick overview of the touring areas, walks and picnic places *in both volumes*. At the start of each tour we refer to the relevant Michelin touring map(s), which are so handy to use in conjunction with their *Red Guide*. *Important: Both driver and navigator should look over the latest Michelin Red Guide before entering or leaving any large city,* so that you have some idea of where you are heading and the landmarks en route. It is *never* as simple as it looks on the touring maps, and *hours* can be wasted twirling in spaghetti loops on ring roads round cities like Aix!

The **touring bases** are, obviously, just *suggestions,* and the tours can be joined at any point en route (the major villages are shown at the top of each tour). Since some of the territory covered is well away from popular tourist areas, we chose bases which offered not only hotels, but *our* essential requirements for making an early-morning start: a petrol station and a mini-market! In many cases, however, we broke the tours to spend a night or two at one of our favourite hotels near a walk — like the top-class château at Trigance or the more modestly priced Trois Vallées at the Col de Turini.

Because this is a *countryside* guide, the tours often bypass the villages en route, however beautiful or

Olive trees below Sigale (Car tour 7)

historically important. We do, however, use symbols to alert you to the cultural highlights (a **key to the symbols** used is on the touring map).

Some other points to keep in mind: **petrol stations** are often closed on Sundays and holidays in the remote areas covered by some of the tours. **Cyclists** do *not* travel in single file, nor is cycling confined to weekends. But on Sundays some roads will be closed off for cycle races: you will have to take a short *déviation*. *Déviations*, however, may *not* be short when they involve road-works. Especially in spring, long stretches of road will be closed, and you may have to go up to 50km out of your way! French **arrow signposting** can be mystifying until you get used to it.

You may note discrepancies in **road numbering**: in a move towards regionalisation, responsibility for most roads has been devolved to local authorities a decade ago. Thousands of roads were renumbered, even iconic trunk roads like the old N85 (Route Napoléon)! But some work is still ongoing.

Finally, remember that **Sundays and holidays** are a nightmare at the most popular 'sights', and places like the Grand Canyon du Verdon and Madone d'Utelle should be avoided. Our tours have been planned not only to take you on the most beautiful roads, but to reach the three-star attractions before or after the crowds. If you follow our advice, but you *still* encounter crowds, we have to admit: we never tour Provence in July or August.

Tour 1: THE CORNICHE D'OR AND THE ESTEREL

Nice • Antibes • Cannes • Massif de l'Esterel • Nice

174km/108mi; 5-6h driving;
Michelin map 341.
Walks en route: 5-7, also
many other walk combinations
in the Esterel (see text below
and map pages 88-89); Walks
1-4 and 8-10 are easily reached
from Nice.
This tour assumes an early
morning start, so that the red
rock of the Esterel can be seen at
its best with a low sun rising in
the east (and so that the busy
coastal roads will be less crowded).
Be sure to fill up with petrol before
turning into the Esterel, and
have your picnic with you. The
short road to Mont Vinaigre is
narrow and not built up at the
side.
Picnic suggestions: There are
good picnic places *all over* the
Esterel, but particularly
pleasant settings are the lake
near the Grenouillet ford (just
as you start into the massif;
rocks to sit on and some shade)
or the dam 30 minutes along
Walk 5 (photographs page
87).

T his tour skirts our favourite stretch of coast in the
south of France; it wins — by a nose — over the
Riviera proper (Nice to Menton, Tour 2). This may be
because it is less built up, but what stays in the memory
are the turquoise-to-jade creeks (*calanques*) below the
road, pierced by blades of crimson rock. Beyond Cap
d'Antibes, we come upon the glorious sweep of the
Golfe de la Napoule and then follow the Golden
Corniche above these *calanques*. Heading inland, we
climb into the 'rock garden' of the Esterel, where
spring-flowering *maquis* and lime-green pines shimmer
against yet more fiery-red porphyry rock.

Leave **Nice** *on the* D6098
(coastal road to ANTIBES*), then*
follow signs for CAP D'ANTIBES.
One could easily spend half a
day at **Antibes★** (15km
i✝✹M♨); save Antibes and
other towns along the coast for
another day, when you could
easily visit by public transport
and not have the hassle of
finding a parking space.
You round the small peninsula
of **Cap d'Antibes★**, with its
luxury hotels, immaculate
gardens and fine coastal views
(*📷*). This road rejoins the
main coastal road at **Juan-les-**
Pins (*i*). After rounding the
Pointe de la Croisette (*📷*)
you come to **Cannes★** (33km
i✝✹✹M♨) and the beautiful
sweep of the **Golfe de la**
Napoule. Save at least a day
for your visit to Cannes.
Beyond **La Napoule** (*i✹M♨*),
now following the **Corniche**
d'Or (Golden Corniche), you
skim past one resort after
another.
Walk 6 begins and ends at
Théoule-sur-Mer (*✹✹♨*),
coming back into the village
via the viewpoint at the **Pointe**
de l'Aiguille (*📷*). The
honeycombe of **Port-la-**
Galère snuggles into terraces
bordering the bay. It is worth
stopping at the **Pointe de**
l'Esquillon★ (*📷*) for the fine
views of the coast all the way
back east to Cap d'Antibes.
The red porphyry cliffs of the

12

Top: the red porphyry rock of Cap Roux (top); boars near the Roussiveau Forestry house. See also photographs on page 87.

Esterel rise up to the right. You pass **Miramar** and then **Le Trayas**, a strung-out settlement on wooded slopes beside the sea. Now the sharply-indented *calanques* create a breathtaking landscape down to your left. Just beyond the **Pointe du Cap Roux** there is an especially fine viewpoint (☞) over this setting at the **Pointe de l'Observatoire★**. Beyond **Anthéor**, at **Agay** (64km *i*☞), we leave the coast to delve into the **Esterel Massif★**.

At the roundabout, turn right on the D100 for VALESCURE* and, 1.6km uphill, fork right on a narrow tarmac road (small brown sign: MASSIF DE L'ESTEREL).

Cap Roux dominates the landscape on the right, as you pass to the left of the **Maison Forestière du Gratadis**.

At the Y-fork, go right for PIC DE L'OURS (perhaps refer now to the large-scale map on pages 88-89).

You ford the **Grenouillet** stream; a lovely lake is on the left here.

At the next junction (Carrefour de Mourrefrey), keep straight ahead for PIC DE L'OURS, where the Cap Roux road comes in from the right (signposted to the Rocher de St-Barthélemy).

Cap Roux rises brilliantly above you here. Travelling on the north side of St-Pilon and

---

But for Walk 7, continue for 2km to the WWII monuments at* **Cap du Dramont, *where you can park.*

Cap Roux, you come to the **Site de la Ste-Baume**, from where footpaths lead up to a cave-chapel dedicated to St-Honorat (waymarked with a chapel 'symbol'; 1h return) and a viewing table on the summit of Cap Roux (2h circuit; 'rocks' symbol). The paths are shown on the map on pages 88-89, but *beware:* they are quite strenuous, vertiginous in places, and not recommended on windy days.

There are fine views to the sea as you climb through an extraordinary landscape of rounded red rock hills freckled with *maquis*. At the **Col de l'Evêque** you head right into a one-way system, continuing round the Pic d'Aurelle to the **Col des Lentisques** (footpath to the summit of Pic d'Aurelle; ☞ 45min return).

Turn right at the col.

Splendid coastal views unravel as you climb, and there are ample opportunities to park. Red rock falls away straight below you, and you look out over the Corniche d'Or all the way back to Cap d'Antibes. Le Trayas is framed by the tip of Point Esquillon, and the Lérin Islands shimmer in the mirror of Napoule Bay.

At the **Col Notre-Dame** (76.5km), the GR51 off to the right leads to the summits of the Petites and Grosses Grues (☜ 1h30min return). You could also climb to Pic de l'Ours (☜ 1h30min return); these routes are shown on the map on pages 88-89.

The main tour turns back south from this pass; keep right, into the one-way system at the **Col des Lentisques**. Once back at the **Col de l'Evêque**, turn right, again on a two-way road. Just under 4km along fork right for MAISON DU GRATADIS, AGAY (the sign may be missing).*

After passing the lake again and crossing the ford, turn sharp right for COL BELLE-BARBE.

Some 400m along, at the **Col de Belle-Barbe**, pull up to park for Walk 5. Or continue straight on. The twin summits of **Perthus** rise ahead on the right. While none of the peaks in the Esterel is very high, the deep ravines, jagged crags and tortuous roads all conspire to convey that enjoyable feeling of being 'in the mountains'.

When you come to the **Col du Mistral** (*beyond which the road*

is closed to motor vehicles), retrace your route via the Col de Belle-Barbe and, at the lake, keep straight ahead, to continue past the Maison Forestière du Gratadis.

At the D100, turn right for VALESCURE/ST-RAPHAEL. Take a km reading here, as your next turn-off is not very obvious. You will follow this road for 6.5km.

Passing small scattered vineyards and new housing developments, keep straight on towards Valescure at the roundabouts. Soon you come into the beautiful **Valescure** golfing development, studded with graceful parasol pines.

After 6.5km along the D100, where a left turn leads to St-Raphaël, turn right on the inconspicuously signposted Route Forestière de la Louve (closed from 9pm to 6am).

There is a dramatic view to Mont Vinaigre from this road.

*At the **Carrefour de la Colle Douce** fork left for LES ADRETS/ DN7. Cross the Pont de la Bécasse and turn right at the T-junction for MONT VINAIGRE.*

Now you have joined the ancient **Via Aurelia** which once linked Rome with Arles via Genoa, St-Raphaël, Fréjus and Aix. Some 3m/9ft wide, it was paved and cambered; as it approached the various staging posts, pavements were raised along the side for pedestrians. Long after Roman times this remained the only road to Italy; today the DN7/D6007 follow much the same route east of Mont Vinaigre. You pass the **Maison Forestière des Cantonniers** on the left — a fit subject for a Utrillo canvas, with its turquoise shutters.

Some 1.5km further on you

But from the Col Notre-Dame one can continue (outside summer) for another 5km to the Col des Trois Termes. After about 2.5km, at the **Col de la Cadière, the GR51 can be followed northeast along the **Sentier des Balcons de la Côte d'Azur**. It is worth walking along this level track for 2km/30min, to the Rocher des Monges, just past the junction for the Col de Théoule. Beyond the Col de la Cadière the road deteriorates and is closed to motor vehicles beyond the Col des Trois Termes, so you cannot drive through to the DN7/D6007.*

Coastal view towards the Golfe de la Napoule and the Corniche d'Or, from the Sentier des Balcons de la Côte d'Azur (possible variation of Walk 6)

come to the **Maison Forestière du Malpey**. Looking at this pretty rose-hued building in idyllic surroundings, it's hard to conjure up the past … the 18th century, when this stretch of the Aurelian Way was the most dangerous spot on the infamous 'Esterel road' and menaced by brigands. Gaspard de Besse (who met an especially grisly death at the age of 25) was the most famous among them; his hideout was a cave in the side of nearby Mont Vinaigre.

At the fork here bear right for MONT VINAIGRE. At the next fork (0.6km) head left (where a track goes right to Plan de l'Esterel and the Aire de l'Olivier). The narrow road is somewhat vertiginous.

There is a typically complex relay station at the parking area and another on the summit of **Mont Vinaigre★** (618m/ 2027ft; 109km), the highest point in the massif and a 200m walk away. From the old watchtower there is a splendid panorama; in the south and east you can trace all of the day's tour.

From Vinaigre return to the Malpey forestry house and turn right. Turn right again at the DN7 (113km).

Some 4.5km after turning onto the D7, you pass to the right of the lovely **Auberge des Adrets** — one of de Besse's favourite watering holes.

*Continue on the DN7/D6007 for 17km, then join the motorway back to **Nice** (174km).*

Tour 2: THE RIVIERA AND THE MERCANTOUR

**Nice • Menton • Sospel • Col de Turini • La Bollène-Vésubie •
St-Martin-Vésubie • Le Boréon • Madone de Fenestre • Vallon
de la Gordolasque • St-Martin-Vésubie**

*216km/134mi; about 12h
driving **over two days**; Michelin
map 341. For day two of the tour
(especially if you plan to walk), it
is very helpful to have IGN map
3741 OT, which you can buy in
St-Martin-Vésubie.*

Walks en route: 8, 9, (10),
11-16; Walks 1-4 are easily
reached direct from Nice.

*As of 2012 many roads on this
tour radiating north from Nice
have been designated 'metropo-
litan', and the yellow-signed 'D'
numbers changed to blue-signed
'M' numbers. This is thought by
some to be a political move (in a
time of austerity!). We have
incorporated the changes which
existed at press date, but the work
is ongoing. Not all road maps will
have yet adopted this blue 'livery'!
St-Martin-Vésubie, halfway
through this tour (109km),
makes a convenient overnight
base. Driving will be very slow
throughout; almost all the roads
are winding. We use three main
access roads into the Mercantour
National Park: the valleys of Le
Boréon, Madone de Fenestre and
the Gordolasque. If you wish to
visit one of the valleys on the first
day of the tour, choose Le Boréon:
it is the shortest, easiest road. All
the roads are good and amply
wide, except in the valley of the
Gordolasque, where the road is
sometimes narrow and not built
up at the side (conversely, in some
places it is very tightly hemmed in
by stone walls). We try to avoid
this road on Sundays/holidays,
when passing can be a nightmare.
There are no petrol stations
between Sospel and La Bollène
(35km) or during the whole of*

*day two in the Mercantour
(107km). Some roads will be
closed from October to May, due
to snow or rock-falls. Note also, if
you plan to walk, that as late as
June snow may still be lying on
the paths we describe; it's a good
idea to check at the National
Park office in St-Martin, to make
sure that you won't need cram-
pons. The refuges should be open
on weekends from April until 15
June, and daily thereafter until
15 September. Do not rely on this;
always carry your own provisions!*

Picnic suggestions: The
chapel steps of **Notre-Dame-
de-la-Menour** north of Sospel
make a fine perch above the
Gorges du Piaon. Almost anywhere during the circuit of the
Authion mountain (optional
detour; see panel on page 23)
you will find grassy slopes or
old ruins to sit on (be sure to
park in a lay-by on this narrow
road). On day two of the tour,
Le Boréon itself is a lovely

Sospel, on the banks of the Bévéra

setting, by the lake or falls, but why not follow Walk 13 to the **Chalet Vidron** (30min), to picnic under fruiting rowans in autumn or to seek out gentians in spring? At **Madone de Fenestre** the grassy slopes near the cross (photograph pages 8-9) give you a superb outlook to the *cirque* or, if you start out on Walk 14, you can picnic overlooking the stream — or up at the lake shown on page 110 (1h on foot). The Gordolasque torrent near the **Pont du Countet** is incredibly beautiful, with the outlook shown on pages 112-114.

First we follow the Grande Corniche above the coast from Nice to Menton, above the fabulous settings of Monaco and Monte Carlo. How many films this conjures up in the mind's eye! How many triumphant roles — and tragedies — have been played out in real life against this backdrop! From the Riviera we quickly climb into the Turini Forest and magnificent firs that would feel at home in Finland. Finally we're in the heart of the southern Alps. Chalets dot the landscape, cow bells ring out, lush green pastureland lies below snow-capped peaks … a Swiss calendar landscape. What surprises most is that we seem to have moved almost effortlessly through three different *countries* in not much over an hour's driving from the coast.

Leave **Nice** by heading east along the Promenade des Anglais: follow road markings for MONACO and MENTON, moving into the left-hand lane. Rise up at the right of the Paillon River and, past the Modern Art Museum, as you approach the large Novhotel, be sure to turn right for MONACO, MENTON PAR GRANDE CORNICHE (D2564).

You quickly climb to the **Grande Corniche★**, originally built by Napoleon along the ancient Via Julia Augusta, the route the Romans first laid down during their campaigns to conquer the Maritime Alps. This magnificent road offers far-reaching views all the way along. Stop first at the **Belvédère d'Eze★** (11km 🎞), from where you look up to the Alps, back to Cap Ferrat and ahead — over the three Corniche roads — to cliffs plunging into the sea. From the **Col d'Eze** (🎞) 1km further on, there is a brilliant view focussing on the church and château in Eze (✕), perched on a rocky spike above the sea — one of most photographed landscapes in France. Some 2km along there is an even finer view back over Eze, with Cap Ferrat, the airport and Cap d'Antibes behind it.

Beyond a road down to Eze, La Turbie suddenly appears ahead: the blinding-white **Trophée des Alpes★** rises behind a church with a cupola of glazed tiles. **La Turbie** (18km �🅿✕M🎞) developed around this fascinating monument. Built in 6BC from almost pure-white local stone, it originally rose to 50m/165ft. It stood on the Via Julia Augusta, in commemoration of Roman victories over 44 different Alpine tribes. Sacked at the end of the Roman Empire, the trophy was mined by the troops of Louis XIV and then used as a quarry (the church incorporates some of its stone); a museum relates its skilful restoration in the early 1900s. Walk 8 begins at La Turbie — a magnificent hike that descends through Eze to the coast.

From La Turbie the road continues below the Monte Carlo radio transmitter on conical Mont Agel.

Head right for MENTON where the D53 goes left to Peille (Walk 3), then go left for ROQUE-BRUNE, MENTON (where the D53 goes right to Beausoleil and Monaco).

Now Cap Martin (Walk 10) is seen ahead. Pull over right in front of the (closed) Vista Palace Hotel at the **Belvédère du Vistaëro★** (23km 🎞), with more fine views to the Italian coast and down over Monaco, with the **Tête de Chien** rising above it.

Curve left in front of the hotel (but then keep right for ROQUEBRUNE, where a left turn goes up to the motorway).

You descend looking ahead to the ancient hill village of Roquebrune. Just 1km after entering **Roquebrune-Cap-Martin★** (24km *i*⛺♨), turn left uphill into the centre. The village has managed to preserve much of its medieval character. The 10th-century fortress, with its castle keep, was erected as a defence against Saracen raids. If you are one step ahead of the coaches, wander through the narrow stepped and covered passageways, with their medieval houses, and soak up the atmosphere which so appealed to Sir Winston Churchill. Walk 10 could begin here.

When you join the M6007 below Roquebrune, turn left for MENTON.

You pass above **Cap Martin★** (Walk 10, photograph pages 98-99) and come into **Menton★** (31km *i*♥✕M♨), sheltered below a backdrop of mountains. Turn right to the seafront, then turn left. There is a pleasant view of the old town as you sweep along the seafront. Park near the 17th-century fort housing the Cocteau Museum (on your right, where the road swings left), if you plan a *quick* visit to the town. Climb up towards the Italianate campanile, where you will come into a delightful square overlooking the coast, the Parvis St-Michel. Two churches open onto this square: the splendid 15/18th-century baroque church of St-Michel and the 17/19th-century Chapel of the White Penitents. More steps will take you up into Rue du Vieux-Château and to the cemetery, from where there is an even finer view over the old town and port. Resolve to return and spend a day here, to see all the museums and gardens. And to do Walk 9, which uses very convenient buses from Menton.

Leave Menton on the D2566 for SOSPEL.

Soon you pass under a very impressive motorway bridge arcing over the valley, through which high mountains are seen ahead. Start climbing in hairpins up the industrialised **Carei Valley**. From **Monti** (halfway along the route of Walk 9) there is a pleasant view across the valley to Castellar (where Walk 9 ends), on a promontory. Beyond a turn-off to Castellar, you begin to climb in hairpins ( ) through the **Forêt de Menton**. The semi-circular **Viaduc du Caramel** is seen on the other side of the valley, and soon you curve past this old railway bridge, built in the 1920s (see page 168).

Keep right at a Y-fork for SOSPEL PAR COL DE CASTILLON.

You pass below **Castillon**, an artists' colony, where the church has a beautiful glazed-tile cupola and much *trompe l'œil* decoration is in evidence. An impressive, deeply-wooded valley is on your left on the climb to the **Col de Castillon**, where you go through a short tunnel.

Beyond the tunnel, turn right on the D2566 for SOSPEL.

Enticing views of the mountains ahead ( ) and olive groves in the immediate vicinity accompany you on the

La Bollène rising above the Vésubie Valley, with the mountains of the Mercantour to the north

spectacular hairpin descent into **Sospel** (49km *i✝☂☂*; Walk 11), where the Renaissance façade and beautiful 10/11th-century Romanesque bell-tower of the classical church (the largest in Alpes-Maritimes) rise high above the surrounding rooftops. Park by the river. Cross the 11th-century bridge shown on pages 16-17; its toll- or watch-tower, which was destroyed in World War II, has been rebuilt and now houses the excellent tourist office. Go ahead to the ancient fountain in the Place St-Nicholas (photograph page 101), then cross back over the bridge and walk to the church square on the right bank, with its beautifully-decorated *trompe l'œil* buildings.

Keeping the river on your right, leave Sospel on the D2566 for COL DE TURINI, MOULINET.

Now you're really *in* the mountains, and the magnificent Authion rises up ahead. Cross the river **Guiou** in a lovely setting of planes and climb the **Bévéra Valley**, passing a waterfall on the right. Soon you're in the **Gorges du Piaon★**, where striated honey-coloured cliffs hang out above you. The road ahead loops ever upwards on stone-built terraces, a 'Great Wall of China' curling lovingly round each limb of the landscape. Watch for the chapel of **Notre-Dame-de-la-Menour** on the right, and park just below it. Don't try to climb to the chapel from here; walk ahead along the road, then steps *on the left* will take you over the pedestrian footbridge to this tiny chapel with its Renaissance façade (✝). Nearby are fine views down to the emerald-green river. **Moulinet**

(70km) is a pretty village in a verdant basin; its church is also stylishly dressed in fashionable *trompe l'œil*.

Nothing quite prepares you for the splendour of the **Turini Forest★**, an enormous mixed woodland blanketing the heights between the Bévéra and Vésubie valleys. Climbing at first through a great variety of deciduous trees with sprinklings of sea pines, you quickly come into the 'real' forest, dominated by larch and magnificent pines. The best time to be here is in autumn, when the delicate red and gold tracery of the deciduous trees is a perfect foil for the towering dark firs — some as much as 50m/150ft high. Bright red berries, thick as cherry clusters, weigh down the rowans.

Four roads converge at the **Col de Turini** (74km *⛰✕*), where Walk 12 begins and ends. It's also one of our favourite places to take a break or stay overnight.

Bear right at the col, then go left on the D70 for LA BOLLENE-VESUBIE. (Or keep straight ahead on the D68, to make a 17km circuit of the Authion★; see box overleaf.)

The D70 descends the valley of the Bollène in hairpins, still buttressed by a 'Great Wall of China'. Not far beyond a tunnel, pull over left at the chapel of **St-Honorat** (✝▭ ☗). From the terrace you enjoy the lovely view shown on page 19. The road descends through chestnut trees, bypassing the centre of **La Bollène-Vésubie** (94km ✝☗), a small hilltop village of 18th-century houses clustered round the church.

Below La Bollène, turn right on

the M2565 (⛽) for ROQUEBIL-
LIERE, BELVEDERE, ST-MARTIN.

Beyond a turn-off left to the
new village of Roquebillière,
look up right to Belvédère,
attractively strung out along a
ridge. Just after this view, you
pass the road to Belvédère and
the Gordolasque Valley (the
66km-point in day two of the
tour, a *very* sharp right turn
from this approach). Now
Mt Tournairet rises on the
other side of the teal-blue
Vésubie River. You pass
below the old part of **Roquebillière**, where the
Romanesque church tower has
a glazed tile cupola. What
strikes the eye immediately is
the colour of the stone in this
area — brown-to-beige, but
strongly streaked with mauve,
burgundy and sienna. Soon
you may notice picnic areas on
both sides of the road (no
tables) bearing a sign, *pacages
interdits* — 'no grazing'. This is
because the traditional *transhumance* (see page 173) is once
again taking place in many
parts of the country. Beyond a
hydro-electric power station
down left, you pass through
Les Châtaigniers (🎐), a
pretty hamlet graced by large
chestnut trees.

As you enter **St-Martin-
Vésubie** (109km *i* ✚ ✕ 🖼), at
the confluence of Boréon and
Madone de Fenestre valleys,
the road makes a tight U-turn
in front of the tourist office
(just where the bulbous tower
of the Chapel of the White
Penitents rises ahead). Park
immediately beyond this turn
and walk to the tourist office;
the office of the Mercantour
National Park (with a small
library) is diagonally opposite.
Both merit a visit before you
explore the town, a good place
to shop for books and maps,
picnics and walking gear. The
12th-century statue of Our
Lady of Fenestre is on view in
the 17th-century church
between October and June; in
summer she resides at the
chapel visited on day two of
the tour.

*On the second day of the tour,
leave St-Martin (0km) heading
north on the main M2565 (the
direction you were heading
when you rounded the tight
U-turn).*

*If you haven't already done so,
fill up with petrol now (⛽).*

*Just over 2km past the petrol
station, turn right on the M89
for LE BOREON.*

It seems as if you have crossed
the border into Switzerland:
alpine chalets dot lush green
pastures. You're following a
15th-century salt route: salt
from the pans at Hyères was
taken by mule via Nice, Utelle
and St-Martin up this valley
and over the mountains into
Italy.

Having crossed the Boréon
stream at Les Trois Ponts (the
Italian border until 1947), you

reach **Le Boréon★** (8.5km ▲✕☍), at the entrance to the **Mercantour National Park**. There's a lovely waterfall and small lake here. Drive ahead through this fairy-tale setting.

At a T-junction, turn right on the D189 (☍), for the VACHERIES DU BOREON.

The road narrows, but is still comfortably wide. The tar ends at a parking area (11.5km ☍).

To park for Walk 13, continue ahead here on a track for another 1km, following PARKING SUPERIEUR DU BOREON.

From the *vacherie* return towards St-Martin.

Just before joining the main road (and just before a bridge), turn sharp left on the AVENUE CHARLES BOISSIER. (There should be a signpost here for Madone de Fenestre.) At the next junction, 1.5km along, bear left on the M94.

As you climb this valley, with the stream on your right, magnificent pines sweep down from the summits of Piagu on the left and Palu on the right. They form a V, and you head straight for craggy **Mont Ponset**, best seen when capped with snow. Some 6km uphill you pass a huge pipe crossing the river at **Les Pontets**; it carries water from the lake at Le Boréon all the way to the power station near Les Châtaigniers. The burbling stream is crossed on a small bridge and, 1.5km further on, you again enter the National Park and pass **La Puncha** on a U-bend (see map page 111). This is also where you should park for Walk 15.

Suddenly you are at **Madone de Fenestre★** (39km ✝), a chapel and the few houses of the French Alpine Club. The magnificent *cirque* shown on pages 8-9 rises before you, dominated by snow-capped **Mt Gélas**. In summer, the chapel with its pretty frescoed walls holds the 12th-century statue of Notre-Dame-de-Fenestre, the object of monthly pilgrimages; in September she is returned to the church at St-Martin (Walk 15 follows this pilgrims' route for part of the way). Walk 14, steeped in history, climbs from here to the Italian border.

*Return to **St-Martin** (51km). Turn left on the main M2565, pass the plane-shaded parking area, round the U-bend and now head south, retracing day one of the tour. Beyond **Roquebillière** bear left on the M71 for BELVEDERE.*

Winding up into Belvédère, ignore two small roads off to the right just before the village. It's worth turning left into **Belvédère** for the view★ (66km *i* ☎) from the post office: you look over the burgundy stone village just below you and down the terraced Vésubie Valley east to the Turini Forest. There is an excellent tourist office here, with a small library.

From Belvédère continue north up the **Vallon de la Gordolasque★**; the road is amply wide *at first,* but it will narrow and become increasingly difficult. From the outset, the surprising absence of pines makes this valley — our favourite — very different from the Boréon and Fenestre. You climb in a bucolic setting past birch and chestnut trees, orchards, and walls built from the gorgeous local mauve-to-purple stone. Be prepared to stop for cows or sheep being led to pasture. Some 7km up

*Consider spending at least half a day exploring the glorious pastures of the **Authion** (see text about the Mercantour National Park on page 73 if you plan to walk). Even if you are not a military history buff, this incredibly beautiful green mountain (see also photograph page 103), riddled with old fortifications, will take your breath away.*

A natural fortress, because of its steep sides and strategic location on the border with Italy, the Authion has twice been the scene of bloody battles. Just after the birth of the French Republic, troops of the Austro-Sardinian coalition occupied the summit, and all Republican efforts to take it failed … until Napoleon took charge. Encircling the mountain with troops (30,000 men were involved in this conflict!), he cut off the enemy's supply lines, winning the County of Nice for the Republicans.

In World War II the Authion was the last place in France to be liberated, only two weeks before the end of the war, after heavy bombardment and a battle lasting three days.

Leaving the Col de Turini on the D68, after 3.5km you come to a monument to those killed in both battles. Bear right at the fork here and follow the one-way circuit, with magnificent views over the Bévéra Valley. There are information panels near the Cabanes Vieilles. When you reach a second monument, park and walk to the fort at the Pointe des Trois Communes, from where you will have a magnificent view over the deep Caïros Valley, across the Mercantour and to Italy. This fort saw the last battle of the Authion; it was taken, surprisingly, by five sailors. When you get back to the war memorial at the start of the circuit, continue back to the Col de Turini and then bear right on the D70 for La Bollène.

from Belvédère, just after crossing a small bridge, look left to the lovely **Cascade du Ray** (📷). Another bridge is crossed about 1km further on; behind it there is a fine view ahead to steep snow-capped peaks, as the valley opens out. The hamlet of **St-Grat** (✕) greets you 2.5km further on, in the setting shown on page 114; its pretty modern chapel is on the left. As you continue below the Cime de la Valette on the left and the Cime du Diable on the right, the valley opens out into wrinkled grassy pastureland strewn with rocks, where the ribbon of river sparkles like tinsel. Just after passing a well-concealed power station, the road ends at a parking area by the bridge shown on page 113 (**Pont du Countet**; 79km). Early in the morning, when the dew drops on the pastures shimmer like diamonds and you are likely to have the rushing stream all to yourself, this valley is an earthly paradise. Walk 16 begins just to the left of the bridge.

Beyond the **Mont du Grand Capelet** rising due east lies the fascinating **Vallée des Merveilles**, where there are more than 30,000 rock engravings dating from the Bronze Age. The valley is an open-air museum, signposted with information panels by the National Park (see 'Note' in the right-hand column on page 112).

*Leaving the bridge, return to the M2565 and bear right, back to **St-Martin-Vésubie** (107km).*

Tour 3: UTELLE AND THE GORGES DU LOUP

St-Martin-Vésubie • Madone d'Utelle • Gorges de la Vésubie • Gorges du Loup • Gourdon • Thorenc

200km/124mi; about 7h driving; Michelin map 341

Walks en route: 17, 18

Roads are good, but narrow and winding. However, a 4.5km-long stretch to Madone d'Utelle is very precipitous and not recommended for nervous drivers or passengers. Avoid this road and the road in the Gorges du Loup on Sundays and holidays. Fill up with petrol before leaving St-Martin (the station is just north of the centre).

Picnic suggestions: *Don't* hope to picnic in the Gorges du Loup; there are very few lay-bys in the prettiest parts of the gorge, and it is always crowded. **Madone d'Utelle** stands on a high plateau with a panoramic view — perfect for picnicking, but note: the road to this chapel is *exceedingly narrow* for a short distance; there is little shade, and sometimes this high ground is populated by more giant ants and crickets than a science fiction film. About halfway through the tour, on the D2 beyond **Coursegoules**, an oak-shaded stretch of road is extremely attractive, and there are grassy terraces to sit on. A little further on, the Chapelle St-Claude just outside **Cipières** offers good parking, a picnic table, shade of cypresses and a wonderful view over the Loup Valley. **Gourdon**, closer to the end of the tour, is the setting for Walk 17: follow it downhill for only five minutes, to a rocky ledge at the top of the trail just visible in the photograph on page 116. There are rocks to sit on, and some shade; the views are just astounding. The **Plateau de Calern**, shown on page 172, is crossed near the end of the tour; it's especially beautiful in spring when the wild flowers are in bloom, and you can park almost anywhere off the side of the wide road (D12). At the end of the tour, two fine choices along the D2: the old ruined village of **Gréolières** and the **Castellaras** (Walk 18), the panoramic viewpoint shown on page 118.

L eaving the pines and sparkling Alpine air of the Mercantour, we head south to the Grasse Pre-Alps, past terraced olive groves. From the *table d'orientation* above Utelle we enjoy one of the finest views in Alpes-Maritimes, before plunging into the Gorges du Loup.

*Head south from **St-Martin-Vésubie** on the M2565.*

You pass below the mellow spread of La Bollène, shown on page 19. At **Lantosque** you cross the Vésubie, continuing on the M2565 (✕ at **Le Suquet**).

*At **St-Jean-la-Rivière** (24km) turn right on the M32 for UTELLE.*

The road climbs in hairpins past drystone walls terracing ancient olive groves. Just as you approach the old fortified village of **Utelle** (32.5km ✝🖼), there is a breathtaking view up the Vésubie Valley to the Mercantour, where the promontory village of La Bollène cuts into the valley like the prow of a ship. Park opposite the main gate, at the viewpoint, and walk into the village, to see St-Véran with its

24

Madone d'Utelle (top) and the Gorges de la Vésubie

fine bell-tower and the charming White Penitents' Chapel.

Then continue uphill, after 1km going left at a fork for MADONE D'UTELLE.

After another 1.5km the road narrows to one threadbare lane. Park at the pilgrimage chapel of **Madone d'Utelle** (39.5km ✝). Legend has it that Iberian sailors, floundering in high seas off Nice, looked up to these heights and saw a light which guided them safely to shore. They founded the chapel in 850, but it was rebuilt in 1806. From here continue ahead to the domed *table d'orientation* ★ (📷), where a wonderful panorama unfolds — from the Alps via the Authion (just behind the chapel) down to Nice, off to Corsica, round to the Esterel and then north over the Grasse Pre-Alps.

Return to the main M2565 (56km) and turn right.

Continue along the steep-sided **Gorges de la Vésubie★**, beside the bounding teal-blue river (various 📷). Some 2km along, just beyond a tunnel, notice the exceedingly sheer walls on the far side of the gorge, the '**Saut des Français**': in 1793 guerillas from the County of Nice hurled Republican troops over these cliffs, just before Nice was reunited with France. Further on, where the Vésubie empties into the river **Var**, Bonson's church rises on the right, at the edge of a pyramidal hill.

*At the roundabout go left for NICE on the M6202; cross the Vésubie on the **Pont Durandy**, with the wide pebbly Var on*

*your right. Some 2.5km along, beyond **Plan-du-Var**, turn right for GILETTE on the M901, crossing the **Pont Charles-Albert**. At the roundabout, take the third exit, the M901 for CARROS.*

The road curls round to where the **Esteron River** also unburdens itself into the Var. At the confluence there is a superb view of the river basin. Just before crossing the Esteron, look up ahead to the perched village of **Gilette**.

At the roundabout on the far side, take the first exit, the M2209 for LE BROC.

25

The pretty little lane climbs through pines and oaks. Soon you pass below the perched village of Le Broc and then go through a short tunnel below Carros.

Some 350m past the tunnel, turn sharp right uphill on the M1 for CARROS VILLAGE and LE BROC. Then follow 'VILLAGE MEDIEVALE' to head up past the château to the top of the village.

This takes you to the *table d'orientation* in old **Carros**★ (81km ■☎), a gorgeous little village surrounding a 13/16th-century château and a wind-mill. From here there is a fine view ahead to Le Broc and towards the scattered perched villages on the east side of the Var. Below, the river fans out round little islets of white pebbles, all the way back to the broad basin where the Var and Esteron converge.

Leave Carros on the M1 for LE BROC.

There's a Mediterranean aroma to the air around here, where scented pines cohabit with aloes, and exotic flowers spill out over balconies and terraces. As soon as you enter **Le Broc**, bear left at a Y-fork for BOUYON (still the M1), leaving the 16th-century church spire off to the right. As you leave, pull up at a lay-by on the right just beyond the cypress-studded cemetery (☎): there are fine views over the Var and the **Chaîne de Férion** beyond it from this cliff-hanging perch. Some 2km from Le Broc, take in one final awesome view (☎) over the industrialised valley and up to Utelle, as well as perched villages left, right and centre.

Then the road goes through an oak wood and the views are lost until, 2km further on, Bouyon is seen across the valley. You cross the river Bouyon and go through the hamlet of **Les Moulins**. Entering **Bouyon** (93km), take the D1 for ROQUESTERON, ignoring the left turn up into the village, with its red-roofed church tower and wrought-iron bell-cage.

At a fork, keep straight ahead for BEZAUDUN on the D8, eventually skirting the Bouyon on the left.

Beyond **Bézaudun-les-Alpes**, which rises off to the right, abandoned terraces flank the road. Ignore two roads up right into Coursegoules; keep straight ahead for GREOLIERES and VENCE, passing verdant rolling fields off to the left.

*After crossing a bridge over the river **Cagne**, turn right on the D2 for GREOLIERES, THORENC.*

Look left soon for a fine view back to Coursegoules, where the 12th-century Romanesque church rises above grassy terraces. Shaded by oaks, this lovely grass-lined stretch of road is very pleasant for picnicking. Soon you look ahead to **St-Pons**, with the bald white summit of Cheiron behind it. The road passes below this hamlet.

At a roundabout where the D3 comes in from Gourdon, go right, to keep on the D2 for GREOLIERES. Then, just 1km further on, bear left on the D703 to CIPIERES.

The road descends in hairpins into the lovely **Loup Valley**, where verdant fields blanket the steep mountainsides.

At a fork after 2.5km, turn right and cross the river, joining the D603.

Cascade de Courmes, in the Gorges du Loup (right); below: carved south door of the church in Le Bar-sur-Loup

Now the walls of the gorge are glimpsed through graceful oaks on the left as you climb. The honeyed huddle of **Cipières** (121km), below a 13/18th-century castle, fans out nicely on the right. Just outside the village you pass the **St-Claude** chapel on the left (⌂), with good parking and fine views. The dramatic road descends again, into a wide, open gorge of honey-coloured rock filled with trees. When the D3 comes in from behind and to the left, join it and continue straight ahead for GOURDON. *Under 2km along*, on a hairpin bend, pull over right at a lay-by with a sign 'Source Parfumée de Gourdon, Point du Vue Panoramique sur les Gorges du Loup': opposite is a short path to a railed balcony (📷), from where the view★ plunges over 350m/1150ft straight down into the Gorges du Loup.

Now go back the way you came for under 2km and, at the junction, bear right with the D3 (GREOLIERES, COURMES).

You descend into the **Gorges du Loup★**.

Just before Bramafan Bridge, turn sharp right, to skirt the river on a narrow two-lane road (D6 to 'BAR S/LOUP').

Under 2km along pull up left to a terraced café, to see the **Saut du Loup★**, where the Cascade des Demoiselles foams into a huge pothole (nominal admission charge). From here the road goes through a tunnel, then descends through a bower of trees, where high orange-white cliffs tower overhead. You cross the **Pont**

de l'Abîme in an invigorating setting, and then go through a second, tiny tunnel. The pretty **Cascade de Courmes★** (photograph above) is just at the exit, but you must park about 200m further on and walk back. Then the road runs through a longer tunnel, passing the odd lay-by, but the drama is behind you.

At **Pont-du-Loup** turn right on the D2210 for GRASSE, LE BAR-SUR-LOUP and cross the river.

Look right to see the pillars of the old bridge, destroyed in World War II. (*At this junction the D2210 heads east to Tourrettes and Vence, but these busy villages are best visited early in the day, direct from the coast.*) Entering **Le Bar-sur-Loup★** (*i*☂️🍴📷), turn right for 'CENTRE VILLE', to climb into the village. Park in front of the huge, squat 16th-century tower (tourist office). Visit the 15th-century Gothic church, with its beautifully-carved south door. At the left of the church is a magnificent viewpoint over the Loup Gorge.

Return to the D2210 and continue south. At **Châteauneuf-Pré-du-Lac**, go sharp right on the D3 for GOURDON (just before a roundabout).

Now the D3 affords splendid views (📷) to the Loup Gorge, Le Bar and magnificently-sited **Gourdon★** (153km *i*🍴M; photograph page 116). Park below the village, where Walk 17 begins and ends.

From the roundabout below Gourdon follow 'CAUSSOLS'.

The wide, little-used road (D12) climbs to a plateau, with fine views (📷) back over Gourdon and down to the coast.

Ignore the narrow Chemin des Claps off left* to an amateur observatory. At the **Col de l'Ecre**, the road sweeps 90° left.

After 3km the D12 sweeps left again; you pass below an observatory and cross the **Plateau de Calern** on a wide grass-lined road, a delight of wild flowers in spring.

Beyond **Caussols**, turn right on the D112 for ANDON, THORENC. When you meet the D5 go right for THORENC, GREOLIERES.

From the **Col de la Sine** (📷) there are spectacular views towards the bright-white **Montagne de l'Audibergue**.

When you cross the **Pont-du-Loup**, ignore the road straight ahead for Andon. Turn right for THORENC, GREOLIERES, then fork right downhill on the D79 to Gréolières.

Skirting the Loup, this road takes you to the attractive village of **Gréolières**.

Before the village centre, follow signs for THORENC (D2).

Heading east above Gréolières, there is a splendid picnic spot at the ruins of the original hamlet. This magnificent high-level road above the Loup Valley is a dramatic run through tunnels laced with viewpoints (📷). Some 7km along you have the option of a 22km return detour to the summit of **Cheiron** (signed to GREOLIERES LES NEIGES). Note the D5 coming in from the left 4km past the Cheiron turn-off: 0.6km futher on, you could park on the left for Walk 18.

Take the next right turn, the D502, into **Thorenc** (200km).

---

*This is an even more attractive route across the plateau than the D12, but *very narrow* (avoid on Sundays when cyclists and para-gliders are out in force). You could follow it via **Les Claps** back to the D12 (past the *borie* shown on page 172). At the D12 turn right towards CAUSSOLS, but then fork left at the next junction (D112), to rejoin the tour on the D5 towards THORENC.

Tour 4: IN NAPOLEON'S FOOTSTEPS

Thorenc • Mons • Fayence • Bargemon • Gorges de Pennafort • Bagnols-en-Forêt • St-Cézaire-sur-Siagne • St-Vallier-de-Thiey • Route Napoléon • Thorenc

203km/126mi; about 8-9h driving; Michelin map 341
Walks en route: 18-22
All the roads are good, but some are narrow. On a short stretch of single lane road between Callian and St-Cézaire there are few passing places. Fill up with petrol at Thorenc or Fayence.
Picnic suggestions: About halfway through the tour you come upon a red-rock landscape reminiscent of the Esterel; it runs between the **Pennafort** and **Blavet gorges**. The best picnicking along this 17km-long stretch is just after you cross the river Endre, in a setting of parasol pines or cork oaks. At the end of the tour, the chapel of **Notre-Dame-de-Gratemoine** on the Route Napoléon is a superb setting for an evening picnic.

While this circuit in the Grasse Pre-Alps takes in some fine perched villages and pretty gorges, two landscapes are likely to linger in your memory: the red-rock world beyond Pennafort and your ascent of the magnificent Route Napoléon below the white Malay, Lachens and Audibergue mountains. Below the village of Séranon you come upon the brave old chapel below,

Notre-Dame-de-Gratemoine on the Route Napoléon below Bauroux.

standing in total isolation below the glowering heights of Bauroux. The austere beauty of this setting, especially at sunset, is overwhelming.

*From **Thorenc** return to the D2 and head east towards GREOLIERES.*

The relay on the Col de Bleine is seen up to the left, while ahead on the right an old ruin rises on a thimble of rock. Watch for a small iron cross on the right 1.2km along; 200m further on you could park for Walk 18, to the ruined **Castellaras** atop the rocky crag.

Just 0.6km further on turn right on the D5 for ANDON.

At the **Col du Castellaras** () there is a fine view along the Loup Valley and over to the snowy-white Audibergue.

*Turn right on the D79 for ANDON and L'AUDIBERGUE. Beyond **Andon**, at the roundabout, continue towards CAILLE (still D79).*

Ahead is an appealing, 'sugar loaf' mountain — the eastern flanks of the mighty **Bauroux**. When you are just below it, at a fork, keep straight ahead into **Caille**. Walk 22 drops down into Caille (literally) after storming the Bauroux summit, but Short walk suggestion 3 on page 125 is a delightful, easy ramble from Caille.

Keep following GRASSE until you reach the D6085 (20km). Turn left for GRASSE; then, 2.5km

*along (at the **Col de Valferrière**), go right on the D563 for MONS.*

The limestone edge of the **Audibergue** rises on the left here, and you look ahead to the **Montagne de Malay**. Soon you enter **Var**, and a verdant basin opens up ahead below the **Montagne de Lachens**. Pines and oaks accompany your descent into the **Vallon du Fil** until, just before Mons, you enjoy a fine view across terraces to the Audibergue and down right to the village.

Lovely grassy fields and plane trees welcome you into **Mons★** (35.5km *i* ). Park in the main square with its 18th-century fountain, tourist office and *table d'orientation*, from where there is a superb view down over the Siagnole Valley (Walk 19). The Audibergue rises to the left, and the vista sweeps round past the high-rise flats in Grasse to the Alps and — on clear days — across the Mediterranean to Corsica. Leave Mons the way you came in, passing to the left of the 15/17th-century church with its bell-cage.

Montagne de Brouis from the Route Napoléon

Fountain at St-Cézaire-sur-Siagne

*Just as you are leaving, turn
right on the D56 for CALLIAN,
ST-CEZAIRE.*

The road bends left, then right.
Pull up right opposite a chapel,
from where there is a fine view
back to Mons. Then the pretty
little road zigzags through
holm oak, with views down to
the Mediterranean.

*After 4.5km keep right with the
D56 ('CALLIAN'), where the
D656 goes left to St-Cézaire.*

Terraced hillsides splashed
with fig trees and olives groves
grace this single-lane road, as
you head towards the
Montagne de Malay. If you are
planning to do Walk 19, park
just before or after the bridge
over the Siagnole (some 2km
from the St-Cézaire turn-off).
Otherwise carry on and, 0.5km
further on, watch out on the
left for a sign alerting you to
the **Roche Taillée★** (**Π**;
photograph page 120). There
is no parking here; you must
pull up where you can and
walk back.

*At a T-junction, turn right on
the D37 for FAYENCE.*

The road passes to the left of
the **Château de Beauregard**.

*On meeting the D563, turn left
for FAYENCE.*

As you approach the village,
you are heading straight for the
Esterel, and spikes of cypresses
pierce the landscape. You pass
to the right of the 18th-century
classical church in the large
village of **Fayence** (55.5km
i♒). Follow TOUTES DIREC-
TIONS. As you curl downhill
out of Fayence (🚽), there is a
beautiful view to the right over
fields.

*Come down to a roundabout
some 2km from Fayence and*
*turn right on the D19 for
SEILLANS.*

Beyond the Romanesque
chapel of **Notre-Dame-de-
l'Ormeau** you come into the
pink- and honey-hued village
of **Seillans** (*i*✝🍴), with an
11/15-century Romanesque
church and a castle.

*From Seillans take the D19
towards BARGEMON.*

There are fine views over a
series of green basins. Then a
lovely forest of oak and sweet-
scented pines takes you almost
all the way to **Bargemon**
(75km *i*✝🍴☐♒). This ancient
village is a good place to shop,
amidst the shady squares and
bubbling fountains. Take time,
too, to see the 12th-century
fortified gates, 15/17th-century
church, the ruined castle, and
the 17th-century chapel of
Notre-Dame-de-Montaigu
with its Gothic spire.

*From Bargemon follow CALLAS
(D25).*

There is a good view to the
houses sheltering below the
ruined castle on your approach
to **Callas** (*i*☐♒), from where
you follow DRAGUIGNAN and
LE MUY (still the D25),
eventually driving between

vineyards and crossing the D562.

You pass an isolated hotel on the right just before the red-rock **Gorges de Pennafort★** on the left. (Just 120m *before* the hotel, opposite a parking area, a path by a tiny sign leads into this beautiful gorge.) The next 17 kilometres take you through some of the most beautiful landscapes in the region, with frequent lay-bys (☎) and places to picnic. Although this area isn't mentioned in most tourist guides, wine-lovers flock to the various *domaines* en route (photograph below), to sample their Côtes de Provence.

At the roundabout on the D47, take the third exit for BAGNOLS.

Beyond a forest of graceful umbrella pines, you cross the river **Endre** and come into a 'museum' of cork oaks and fabulous views down to the coast. The rosy brushstrokes culminate in a final flourish at the **Gorges du Blavet** (☐; Walk 20 could begin here), beneath stipples of purple-flowering heather and metallic-leaved holm oaks.

Soon Bagnols spreads out ahead on the right. The access road to Walk 20 turns off to the right at the **Chapelle Notre-Dame**, just before the wine cooperative.

At a junction, turn left for FAYENCE.

You climb through pretty plane-shaded **Bagnols-en-Forêt** (112km *i*) and leave it on the D4, with good views ahead to the mountains where the tour began — Malay, Lachens and Audibergue.

*Ignore the D56 right to Callian; keep left for FAYENCE, ST-PAUL-EN-FORET. In **St-Paul-en-Forêt**, keep right on the D4 for FAYENCE, GRASSE. After 5km, at the roundabout, turn right for GRASSE (D562).*

Soon there is a fine view ahead to the two square towers of Tourrettes, with Fayence to the left. The road skirts to the right of an aerodrome.

Coming to a roundabout with the Marché Paysan on the left, take the third exit for CALLIAN.

Colle Rousse (Walk 20) and vine-yard near the Gorges de Pennafort

Callian, crowned by its castle, now rises on a hill to the right, with Montauroux beyond it. Cypresses, olive groves and salmon-coloured rooftops enhance the climb towards **Callian** (131km ♣♿). You pass below the 15/17th-century château and to the right of the 17th-century church with glazed tiles on the tower.

Outside Callian, turn left on the D37 for MONS.

There is a lovely view of Callian down to the left.

Just over 0.5km along, turn right on the D96 for ST-CEZAIRE.

Soon there is a fine view right towards St-Cézaire, as you start up the valley below the towering walls of the **Gorges de la Siagne**★, with the Audibergue ahead. Some 6.5km along you cross the Siagnole. Ignore the D656 left to Mons here: keep ahead and cross the Siagne, at the same time entering **Alpes-Maritimes**. Now go down the other side of the gorge, at the base of the escarpment, on a good, two-lane road (D105). Climb in zigzags through terraced olive groves into **St-Cézaire-sur-Siagne**★ (144km *i*♣⌕), and follow *CENTRE VILLE* to park in this medieval perched village with a fine 13th-century cemetery chapel (where Walk 21 begins). From the church you can follow a path to a *table d'orientation*. (The famous **Grottes de St-Cézaire** are 4km northeast of the town, on the D613.)

Leave St-Cézaire on the D5 for ST-VALLIER.

Again heading towards the Audibergue, you come into **St-Vallier-de-Thiey** (153km *i*♣♿), a former Roman

stronghold and a pleasant holiday resort. A 12th-century church is adjacent to the castle housing the town hall.

On meeting the D6085 turn left for CASTELLANE.

This is the **Route Napoléon**★, climbed by the Emperor on his return from exile in Elba in March 1815, when he headed for Grenoble and an uncertain future. To avoid the main roads (guarded by troops loyal to the king), his small band used what was then a steep, muddy mule trail. From the **Pas de la Faye**★ (159.5km ⌕) there are superb views to the south — from La Napoule Bay to the Maures. Beyond **Escragnolles** the Audibergue peters out on the right, in a final curtain of cliffs. At the **Col de Valferrière** you pass the D563 to Mons driven earlier. Drystone walls terrace the approach to **Séranon**, where you come upon the **Chapelle Notre-Dame-de-Gratemoine** (see page 29). Short walk 22-2 can begin here, but the main walk begins in the village up to the right. Just 1km beyond the chapel, watch for the exquisite sign on Séranon's old post office, on the left (photograph page 1). Beyond here the grandeur of the road ends in a jumble of touristic sites, shattering the illusion of marching with history.

At **Le Logis-du-Pin** (186km) you cross the Artuby.

Turn right on the D2211 for ST-AUBAN; 2.5km along, take the D2 right for THORENC.

This road skirts to the left of the clover-green **Lane Valley** shown on pages 126-127).

After 13.5km turn left on the D502 to **Thorenc** *(203km).*

Tour 5: LAC D'ALLOS

Thorenc • Castellane • St-André-les-Alpes • Colmars • Lac d'Allos • Colmars

123km/76mi; about 5h driving; Michelin map 341
Walks en route: 23; Walk 28 is nearby.
All the roads are good, but it's a slow pull up to the parking area for the Lac d'Allos (be sure you have enough petrol before starting on this road). Some passes may be closed between October and May.
Picnic suggestions: The **Lac de Castillon**, shown on page 143, is popular with picnickers, and there is ample parking by the dam or, further on in the tour, at **St-André** (⊼).

Beyond St-André, when you are skirting the Verdon, the ruined hamlet of **Plan de Lys** and the old **Pont d'Ondre** (shown opposite) are pleasant perches overlooking the river. But the best picnic spots on this tour are at the **Lac d'Allos**: by lake itself (photographs pages 129, 130) or near the parking area — either where the Chadoulin weaves a meander through the meadows (photograph page 36) or where willows edge the Méouille (page 129).

W e skirt one of the loveliest man-made lakes in the south of France, before following the Verdon upstream towards its source near the Col d'Allos. But the highlight of the tour is the magical setting of the Lac d'Allos — the largest natural lake in Europe above 2200m. Don't expect to see it from your car; it's a good half hour away. And while you're making the effort, *don't* just follow the crowds straight to the lake; do Short walk 23!

From Thorenc take the D2 west towards the D6085.

The road skirts the Lane Valley on the left (photograph pages 126-127). The mountain of Bauroux appears ahead (its summit, which towers above the Route Napoléon on Car tour 4, is the goal of Walk 22). Ignore the turning left to Caille; keep ahead past the hamlet of **Valderoure** and the pretty farm of **Malamaire** with its chapel.

Fork left on the D2211 for GRASSE.

After 2.5km you meet the Route Napoléon (D6085; see Car tour 4) near the setting shown on page 30.

Turn right for CASTELLANE.

Just as you come into

Castellane (34km; see notes on pages 46-47), look out on the right for the beautiful 17th-century bridge over the **Verdon**. Then cross the new bridge and, if you are stopping, take the second right turn after the bridge, to park in the Place Sauvaire.

From Castellane follow DIGNE, to continue north on the D4085. The road climbs to a roundabout, where you take the second exit, the D955 for ST-ANDRE and ANNOT.

Soon you begin to skirt the **Lac de Castillon★**, a gorgeous drive. Pull over at one of the large parking areas just before or after the 100m/330ft-high dam between this lake and the smaller, milky-green **Lac de Chau-danne** (🕮 with information panels). At 42km you pass the VC5 back right to Demandolx (Car tour 7 and Walk 28); keep ahead for ST-ANDRE, making for the salmon-coloured rooftops of St-Julien. *On meeting the N202, turn left.*

You pass to the right of **St-Julien-du-Verdon**, a water-sports centre. Ignore the road right to Angles; keep left, crossing the **Verdon** once more. Near the top of the lake, just as you enter **St-André-les-Alpes** (54km *i*🚠), there is a large parking area (🕮🏂) from where you can watch the para-gliders based on the far side — below *robines* (clay slopes) running down the hillside in pleats. As well as being a world-famous mecca for para-gliders, St-André is a fruit-growing area and a well-sited tourist centre.

Leave St-André on the D955 for COLMARS, COL D'ALLOS.

You soon cross the river **Issole**. This very pleasant road

sees little traffic. As you approach **La Mure** the *robine*-etched valley of the Verdon is close by on the right. Beyond a stretch of woodland, about 10km from St-André, the valley opens out, with invigorating views of the rushing river and verdant fields running down off the mountains. With luck you'll spot the Train des Pignes (see page 168) along here, and give it chase!

After crossing the Verdon you are in the upper valley (various 🕮), and green fields take you into **Thorame-Haute-Gare**. Some 2km further on, opposite the KM4 road marker, the impressive ruined hamlet of **Plan de Lys** on the left is a delightful grassy picnic spot overlooking the river. You pass the hamlet of **Font-Gaillard** and then cross the Verdon yet again at **Pont de Villaron**. Some 0.5km after crossing the bridge, look down right to a most beautiful setting — over the old **Pont d'Ondre** shown below. To picnic here, pull

The old Pont d'Ondre over the Verdon north of Pont de Villaron

Short walk 23 diverts to a plateau below Mont Pélat (left), before going on to Lac d'Allos. Everyone rushes past the meandering Chadoulin stream (below) in their haste to get to the lake (shown on page 130), but it's our favourite place to linger. Below right and bottom: Colmars, the church and the Fort de Savoie.

over at the ruined building beside the road.

Having joined the D908, you enter a defile of honey-coloured cliffs and make straight for the snow-capped Alps (📷). After a straight stretch of tree-lined road, where false acacias and birches are prominent, you pass to the right of the pretty summer resort of **Beauvezer**.

Swiss-style chalets dot the landscape before **Colmars** (83km *i* ✝ ⛺ 🚿), which is approached along a lovely avenue of chestnuts. Notice the sundial on the Porte de France, at the southern entrance to this old fortified town. The parking area is further north on the main road; nearby are the tourist office and Fort de Savoie. The 16/17th-century Romanesque/Gothic church is near the gate with the sundial.

As the road curves past the Fort de Savoie follow COL D'ALLOS.

The heavily-restored 13th-century Romanesque chapel of **Notre-Dame-de-Valvert** (✝) is on your left as you enter **Allos** (91.5km 🚿).

Just 100m beyond the chapel, turn very sharp right on the D226 for LE VILLARD, LAC D'ALLOS.

Now you climb in hairpins past solitary farms, up the most westerly valley of the **Mercantour National Park**, towards the pyramid of Mont Pélat. Rowans and graceful pines trace the Alpine landscape. The zigzags give fine views back over Allos, in a green basin backed by high mountains but, sadly, most of the old-style larch-shingle roofs have been replaced by corrugated iron. Beyond the **Ravin de Valplane** you enter the National Park, climbing beside the **Chadoulin** torrent. On reaching the parking area for the **Lac d'Allos**★ (103km), turn to page 128.

*From Allos retrace your route back to **Colmars** (123km).*

Tour 6: GORGES DU CIANS

Colmars • Col des Champs • Beuil • Gorges du Cians • Puget-Théniers • Entrevaux • Annot • Thorenc

181km/112mi; about 5-6h driving; Michelin map 341
Walks en route: 24-26; Walk 28 is on the alternative return route.
The tour follows many narrow winding roads; none is vertiginous, but you may have to back up a considerable distance if you meet oncoming cars. Some passes may be closed between October and May. Fill up with petrol before leaving Colmars.
Picnic suggestions: You *could* picnic in the Cians Gorge, but only on one of the busy public walkways — pity, but there are other fantastic settings on this tour. Early on, the **Col des Champs** is a weird but incredibly beautiful setting of *robines* (black clay slopes) covered with grass. There is no

shade at the col but, beyond it, when you are below tree-line, you can picnic on grassy banks, under pines. At **Beuil** you could either follow Short walk 24 or picnic by the St-Ginié chapel, a short detour off the D28 (photograph pages 132-133). Notre-Dame-de-Vers-la-Ville at **Annot** (Short walk 26) is a very pleasant setting with ample shade. As you approach Vergons, near the end of the tour, you will spot the apse of **Notre-Dame-de-Valvert**, a Romanesque chapel in a field on the right; it's a lovely setting, but there is no nearby shade. If you take the alternative return route via the D102, consider an evening picnic at **Ville** (see Car tour 7 and Walk 28).

A fter an exhilarating run across high alpine pastures, we descend *the* most spectacular gorge in Provence — the Gorges du Cians, with Permian schists ranging in colour from pale pink through wine red to dark purple. Magical Entrevaux and three or four delightful walks lie en route.

Head north from Colmars on the main D908, then fork right on the D2 for COL DES CHAMPS.

You may see a sign here, 'Interdit aux troupeaux': it simply means that no livestock may be driven along the road; see *Transhumance*, page 173. This *very narrow* road climbs in hairpins; through the trees you can glimpse the upper Verdon Valley, pastureland and high mountains. Some 4km uphill you could park and walk to the **Panorama de la Collette** (⌖ 30min return), a viewpoint over the Verdon and Lance valleys. Another 1.5km brings you to the **Site Nordique de**

Ratéry (⌖) and a fine view left to Allos, then you continue through majestic pines. Before you've noticed it, the landscape changes totally, and you look left towards a 'bulldog's-face' of furrowed slopes — grass-covered *robines* — weird, but incredibly beautiful pastureland (various ⌖).

More charcoal-black clay slopes (see photograph on page 173) edge the road at the **Col des Champs★** (2087m/6850ft; 12.5km ⌖), from where there is a magnificent view to the encircling peaks, often dusted with snow.

Beyond the pass the road

becomes the D73, as you leave Alpes de Haute-Provence for **Alpes-Maritimes**. Now two lanes wide and lined with gold grasses and mullein, the road descends below the needle-sharp **Aiguilles de Pelens** into the tree-line. You pass an isolated *auberge* on the left and then, about 10-11km down

from the pass, the sweet little chapel of **St-Jean** on the left, with a larch-shingle roof.

Just past the chapel, at a fork, go right on the D78 for LE MOUNARD and SUSSIS.

This country lane threads its way past abandoned hamlets and neglected orchards. After

Cians Gorge — the Grande Clue

4.5km, where the D278 comes in from the left, there is a beautiful view of the upper Var Valley and the mountains behind it, as you approach St-Martin — seen down to the right.

In the attractive resort of **St-Martin-d'Entraunes** *(28.5km) go right on the D2202 for VILLENEUVE, GUILLAUMES.*

The road, at first lined with fine-leaved poplars, crosses the river **Var**, then runs between orchards. Just past **Villeneuve-d'Entraunes** mountains and *robines* fall away to the left in tiers. Soon the Var is a mass of stones on your right, and you cross the river **Barlatte**. Beyond the hamlet of **La Ribière** lies the first of the tunnels cut into the jagged mountain that dominates **Guillaumes** (40km *i*✦⬚), a very pleasant tourist centre with a ruined castle and Romanesque church.

On the far side of Guillaumes go left on the D28 for VALBERG. *

The good road traverses a chaos of rock, interspersed with pines and the occasional green field. Some 4km beyond the hamlet of **St-Brès**, at the **Col de Valberg** (📷) you look out left over the verdant basin of the **Alpreyt** stream and right over **Valberg** (53.5km *i*), a skiing resort best seen from a distance — or in winter. Bear right at the roundabout in front of the church here for *BEUIL*, still on the D28. From **Les Launes** there is a good view right to **Beuil** (✦✕⬚) — gateway to the Cians Gorge.

There is a 15/17th-century church and Renaissance White Penitents' Chapel with a fine *trompe-l'œil* façade in the village, where Walk 24 begins.

Leave Beuil on the D28 for TOUET S/VAR, NICE, GORGES DU CIANS.

Look back to Beuil's magnificent setting★ as you descend below tall flint-grey houses perched above Alpine pastures. Just over 1km along, a left turn signed *'LE CIRIEI'* leads to the St-Ginié chapel, where the photograph on pages 132-133 was taken.

Some 5km below Beuil you enter the red-rock landscape of the upper **Gorges du Cians★**. In its rushing descent of 22km from here to where it bounds into the Var, the Cians drops some 1600m/5250ft, leaving in its wake towering chasms. The most beautiful section of the gorge (and the longest) is the run between Beuil and Pra-d'Astier, where the river cuts through red schist. The contrast between the burgundy rock and the varying greens of the trees, ferns and moss is breathtaking. There is parking (📷) at all the tunnels, where the old road has been made into walkways/viewpoints: watch for signs alerting you to the **Grande Clue** and, not far beyond it, the **Petite Clue** — these are the most spectacular rifts. The red rock ends as abruptly as it began, just before the hamlet of **Pra-d'Astier**, from where you wind down below the steep cliffs of the Gorges Inférieures. Had you not seen the Upper Gorge, you would rate these honey-coloured chasms amongst the most impressive in the south of France.

---

*The Gorges du Daluis, south of Guillaumes, are definitely worth visiting if you have time.

At the D6202 (82.5km), *turn right for* DIGNE, PUGET-THENIERS.

The road, lined with plane trees, follows the upper Var. On the approach to **Puget-Théniers** (*i*♣✕▯♨♨), look up behind the castle ruins to the knife-edged **Castagnet Cliffs** shown on page 136; Alternative walk 25 tackles them in a surprisingly easy series of zigzags. Park in the small plane-shaded square on your right, near Maillol's famous statue, *L'Action Enchaînée*. Perhaps visit the old town and the 13/17th-century

Entrevaux was fortified in the late 17th century by Vauban, who linked the hilltop castle with the lower town, enclosing both in ramparts. You can climb to the ruined fortress for superb views over the village and the Var Valley.

Romanesque church with its poignant calvary. Be sure to call at the excellent tourist office on the other side of the road, and the adjacent railway station, where you can collect timetables for the 'Train des Pignes' (see page 168) and the steam train. Walk 25 is a lovely circuit above Puget-Théniers. Plane trees on the right and a 5km-long tapestry of orchards on the left now take you to magical **Entrevaux★** (*i✝☐⌂⌂*), founded in the 11th century.

To appreciate the site (see page 41), turn left opposite Vauban's gate, then go right on the D610 for PARKING PANORAMIQUE. Almost 2km up this road (where the C3 goes right to BAY), make a U-turn and drive back downhill. After 1km, at a bend, pull over to the right, by a bench (⌨).

Back at the main road, park just opposite the gate (photograph page 170), go over the drawbridge, and explore the ancient village.

Then continue west on the D4202, skirting the Var. After crossing the **Pont de Gueydan** (where the Var has cut the Daluis Gorge on the right), keep left on the N202 for GRENOBLE, DIGNE, ANNOT. Now hemming the river **Coulomp**, you pass a viewpoint (⌨) left over the old Roman **Pont de la Reine Jeanne**. A magnificent bluff rears up ahead on the right: Walk 26 would take you along its rim (see photograph page 139.

*At **Les Scaffarels**, below the bluff, turn right on the D908 for ANNOT.*

The road follows the gentle green valley of the river **Vaïre**. On your right are gigantic boulders, the **Grès d'Annot★**; Walk 26 explores them; see photograph page 138. If you are doing that walk, turn right for GARE just before the centre. Otherwise continue to the main square in **Annot** (114.5km *i⌂⌂*) and park on the left to see the lovely old town.

Return from Annot to the main N202 and turn right.

Under 2km along you edge the steep walls of the **Clue de Rouaine**. Beyond pretty **Rouaine**, the river **Iscle** flows below pleasantly-cultivated rolling hills, as you approach the **Col de Toutes Aures** and the lovely Romanesque chapel of **Notre-Dame-de-Valvert** (✝). At **Vergons**, 2km further on, the **St-Ferréol** chapel perches atop a conical hill (notice its diagonal strata, so characteristic of this area). Beyond the defile of the **Clue de Vergons** you look ahead to the beautiful setting of St-Julien-du-Verdon on the **Lac de Castillon** (photograph page 143).

*At the D955 turn hard left towards CASTELLANE, retracing the outward route of Tour 5 back to **Thorenc** (181km). Or vary the return (provided there are no nervous passengers in the car): 5km along the D955 fork left for DEMANDOLX (VC5; the opposite direction to Tour 7; Walk 28 lies en route). Just before Demandolx, keep right on the sometimes very narrow D102 above the Chaudanne Lake, rejoining the D4085 east of Castellane.*

Tour 7: RIFTS AND RIVER VALLEYS

**Thorenc • Col de Bleine • Aiglun • Sigale • Clue de St-Auban •
Lac de Castillon • Castellane • Comps-sur-Artuby • Tourtour •
Aups**

*176km/109mi; about 7h driving;
Michelin maps 341, then 340*
Walks en route: 27-30
*Two stretches of road are precipi-
tous and not always built up at
the side: the 1km-long climb to
the viewpoint above the Col de
Bleine, and the D110/D10 from
Les Sausses to Sigale. These roads
are only recommended for very
confident drivers, as there are few
passing places. Avoid on weekends
and in July/August. Sound your
horn, too, if you feel uneasy: the
locals do! Otherwise, avoid these
roads altogether: when you
descend from the Col de Bleine,
turn left on the D5 for* ST-AUBAN
*rather than right for Le Mas.
The St-Auban clue is the most
impressive in any case, and you
can pick up the tour there (saving
over 50km). No petrol between
Thorenc and Castellane (97km).*
Picnic suggestions: There are
picnic places galore on this
tour, beginning with the **Col
de Bleine** (shade, rocks to sit
on) at the start. Our favourite
setting in the *clues* is below the
Pont du Riolan, where you'll
see the 'Roman baths' shown
above — but you have to be
very agile to get down to the
river, a popular base for
canyoning. Beyond
Demandolx you can follow
Walk 28 for a short way to
Ville. Or picnic by the shores
of the **Lac de Castillon** itself
(photograph page 143), near
where you cross the dam
(rocks to sit on, shady trees
2km past the dam). We
inevitably make for the settings
shown on pages 6-7, 47 and
51, where it's easy to get down
to the **banks of the Verdon**
(just before the Clue de

*Be sure to pull up at the Pont du
Riolan, a gorgeous picnic spot for
those agile enough to get down to
the river. Can you resist it? The
white limestone basin with its
sculpted strata and milky turquoise
water brings to mind marble
Roman baths. Kayakers are often
seen here, where they meet up after
navigating the Clue du Riolan.*

Chasteuil). The chapels at
Comps (see pages 144-145)
are an attractive setting, but if
you don't have time to walk up
to them, there is another
chapel just 1.8km south of
Comps on the east side of the
D955 (beyond a shrine). Near
the end of the tour, the 5km-
long run through the delightful
mixed woodland of the **Bois
de Prannes** is a good choice,
especially if you have a table
and chairs.

This tour leaps from river to river, as we make our way west to Aups. First we follow the Esteron and its surging tributaries amongst the *clues*, the very deep and narrow rifts they have sliced through the limestone. The kayakers are in their element here, and you may have to compete with them for parking space. We then move on to the Verdon and perhaps picnic on its banks, watching more colourful kayaks whizz by. But we don't venture into the Canyon (Tour 8) today; instead we skirt its idyllic tributary, the Jabron. The Artuby opens our route to the Nartuby and the pretty Gorges de Châteaudouble. Late in the day there's one last chance for a walk — from the delightful hill village of Tourtour.

Head north from **Thorenc**, *to pick up the D5 for COL DE BLEINE (no signposting at time of checking).*

Look back now, down to Thorenc, east to the ruins of the Castellaras, and west to Bauroux.

Some 3.5km from Thorenc, at the **Col de Bleine** *(a popular*

Sigale: the clock tower, from the church square

hang-gliding centre and very busy on Sundays) turn right uphill on a very narrow road; 1km further on, go left (away from the relay).

The road ends at a superb viewpoint★ (📷) south along the Loup and Lane valleys (shown on pages 126-127). In the northeast the relay at Madone d'Utelle stands out against the Alps of the Mercantour.

Descend from the viewpoint and continue over the pass, curling down to the Gironde Valley below the Montagne de Charamel.

At a junction turn right on the D10 for LE MAS, AIGLUN. *After 0.6km, at a Y-fork, bear right on the D110 for LES SAUSSES.*

Round rock turrets rise on the left before you go through the attractive old hamlet of **Les Sausses**. Keep straight ahead on the D110 for LE MAS, AIGLUN.

When you meet the D10 again, turn right for AIGLUN.

The road narrows to a single lane. Now we begin our

---

*Or turn left on the D5, direct to the Clue de St-Auban, the easier route mentioned above.

(sometimes hair-raising) circuit of the *clues*. As you approach the first of them, 3km along, there is a fine view to the right, over the village of Aiglun; beyond it, densely-wooded slopes rise on both sides of the **Esteron Valley**. Now you head in towards the rift, to a tight U-bend, where you cross the Esteron. Although the road is *very* narrow here, if there is no traffic about, pull over. On your left is the blade's-width entrance to the **Clue d'Aiglun★**, an almost 2km-long gash running north between the Charamel and St-Martin mountains. Walk 27 begins at **Aiglun** (27.5km), the pretty eyrie shown on page 140. It looks out across the valley to the Cascade de Végay and the Montagne du Cheiron. Continuing east above the Esteron, you pass below Aiglun's cemetery, where the chapel of Notre-Dame rises on a promontory, surrounded by cypresses. The hamlet of Vascognes lies just below the road a little further on; Walk 27 goes through it (photograph page 142). One can still cross the Esteron footbridge below Vascognes — a most invigorating experience! Now look ahead, to the perched village of Sigale, where the escarpment falls away in 'swirls' of strata down to the river. Some 5km from Aiglun, pull up just before the **Pont du Riolan** (📷), to see the irresistible 'Roman baths' shown on page 43. From here the road curves uphill below Sigale, cuddled into the ridge above the swirling rock. Its 19th-century clock tower, adorned with a bell-cage, stands out against the sky like a chess rook.

Climbing through the olive-planted terraces shown on page 11, you join the D17 and go straight ahead (left) for SIGALE on the good wide road that has come in from Roquesteron. Come into **Sigale★** (37km 📷), a beige and pink sprawl of old houses shaded by planes. Two of the gates to this ancient fortified village are still intact, but what always catches the eye is the clock tower on its isolated rock plinth. You feel really high up here at Sigale, where the precipitous walls fall away to the confluence of the Esteron and Riolan. Continuing west on the D17, a wider road takes you high above green fields to the entrance to the **Clue du Riolan★**, with a view left into this deep gouge across the mountains. Acacias — all the more noticeable when they are pollarded — line the left-hand side of the road as you approach the **Pont des Miolans**.

After crossing the bridge, turn left on the D2211a for SALLAGRIFFON, COLLONGUES.

Not far along, breaks in the dense foliage allow pleasant views to **Sallagriffon** up on the left. Behind it is the bulbous summit of Charamel. Soon **Collongues** reveals itself ahead, rising above verdant fields. As you enter, keep left (no signposting at time of checking).

At the next junction, just over 1km further on, keep ahead on the D2211a for BRIANÇONNET, ST-AUBAN.

The old Roman village of **Briançonnet** (60km 🏛) snuggles below a spit of rock with a ruined castle.

Keep following ST-AUBAN, now on the D2211.

You continue via hairpins up to the **Clue de St-Auban★** (66km). Unlike the previous two *clues*, you don't just pass the entrance to this one — you drive *through it* for 1km (on a good, amply-wide road, with space to park and *savour* the drama). Park at the first tunnel, to follow the railed walkway (📷) and look out at the massive vertical walls pitted with caves, and the boiling torrent below. (The photograph on page 171 was taken here, but there are other parking places *in* this clue and at the end of it, where there is also a ramshackle café.)

Out of the clue fork right for ST-AUBAN; then ignore a road off right to the centre.

Still following the Esteron (D305), gentle tree-clad mountains rise on the left and a honey-hued rock edge on the right. On leaving Alpes-Maritimes for **Alpes de Haute-Provence**, the road becomes the D102, and rolling green fields suddenly appear on the left. Squeeze through the attractive pastel houses of old **Soleilhas** and keep straight ahead on the far side of the village for CASTELLANE. There is a gorgeous view back down to the Alpine setting of Soleilhas as you climb above it.

*On coming to the **Col de St-Barnabé**, go straight over for CASTELLANE, DEMANDOLX.*

This upland road, lined with gold grasses and wild roses, descends through *garrigues* towards the mountains behind St-André and Castellane. Curlicued wrought-iron street lamps line the main road through **Demandolx** (83km

📷), from where there is a bird's-eye view★ down over the milky-green straits of the Lac de Chaudanne. (If you plan to do Walk 28, watch for the sign denoting the exit from Demandolx, and *take a km reading* there; you will want to park exactly 2km beyond the sign.) Not far below Demandolx, you join the C2 and keep straight ahead for ST-JULIEN, CASTELLANE. About 0.5km after crossing an impressive road bridge, pull over left at the small iron **Croix de la Mission**. From this viewpoint★ (📷) you overlook the breathtakingly beautiful Lac de Castillon (photograph page 143), a turquoise mosaic of shadows and reflections. Beyond here, look straight ahead as you go into a deep U-bend: above rise the ruins of Ville, the setting for Walk 28 (park at the U-bend). Now the road curls down to the lake, coming to the D955 just above the red-roofed houses of **La Cité**.

Turn left on the D955 for CASTELLANE.

Under 1km along you come to the first of several parking areas (📷 and information panels) either side of the graceful dam between the **Lac de Castillon★** and the **Lac de Chaudanne★**. If you walk over the dam, you will appreciate its height (100m/330ft) — try not to think about the fact that it is only 26m/85ft wide at its base! Still skirting the lake, you pass some pleasant shady places to pull over for a picnic.

*At a roundabout with the D4085 (**Route Napoléon**; Car tour 4), turn left ('GRASSE' etc).*

In **Castellane** (97km *i*✝⚄) the road heads towards the 14th-century Tour de l'Horloge with its lovely wrought-iron bell-cage and then turns right in front of it. Watch now, on the right, for house No 34 (**M**), where Napoleon rested during his tiring slog up to Grenoble. Park in the central square just ahead (Place Sauvaire), if you plan to visit the town (one of the most popular touring and walking centres in Haute-Provence). It's a steep climb past the Stations of the Cross up to the early 18th-century pilgrimage chapel of Notre-Dame-du-Roc, but you will have a fantastic view over Castellane and the entrance to the Verdon Gorge. Don't miss the lovely 17th-century bridge over the

The Verdon at the Clue de Chasteuil (see also photographs pages 6-7, 51)

Verdon (straight below Notre-Dame). Back near the clock tower you will find the tourist office and 12th-century church of St-Victor. Castellane also marks the eastern end of the 'Route de la Lavande', which extends west to Sault (see *Western Provence*, Car tour 3).

From the roundabout at Place Sauvaire turn right on the D952 for COMPS, MOUSTIERS, now referring to map 340.

As soon as you can, pull over to look back to Castellane's setting, for the fine view★ of the Virgin crowning Notre-Dame-du-Roc. (An *oppidum* once stood atop the rocky pinnacle, but the settlement spread down to the Verdon and was fortified in the 14th century; the clock tower is a remainder of those fortifications.) Now you skirt the glorious turquoise **Verdon River** on your left, past a string of camping and kayaking centres. Notice the 'crown' of dolomitic rock up ahead on the right — the **Cadières de Brandis**. You pass the **Pont de Taloire**, a popular fishing spot, on the left, and then come to the **Porte de St-Jean**, a spectacular defile where the road has been hewn out under cliffs and the river races by hard on the left. About 1km further on, you can park on either side of the road, and it's possible to get down to the river for a picnic in the gorgeous setting shown on pages 6-7, below the Cadières de Brandis. Beyond here the river curves to the south and soon the escarpment of Robion (photograph page 51) rises on the left. Then more cliffs arc over the road as you pass through another dramatic rift in the limestone, the **Clue de Chasteuil**.

*Bear left on the D955 for COMPS, crossing the Verdon on the **Pont de Soleils**.*

Soleils is a charming hamlet in the shadow of Robion. Not far past here, beautifully pollarded chestnut trees appear on the right; they will accompany you much of the way to Jabron. Now **Trigance** (✕), with its 16th-century château-hotel and church tower with glazed tiles, rises on the right (photograph page 53); keep ahead, soon following the green ribbon of the **Jabron Valley** on your right. On entering the mellow cluster of **Jabron** bear right for COMPS (still D955). You climb out of the valley, enjoying a wonderful view back over it 1km outside Jabron (☞). Then, 3km further on, there is another dramatic view — towards **Comps-sur-Artuby** (125km *i*), where the 13th-century church of St-André rises isolated on a hill, above more swathes of emerald cultivation. Walk 29 is a delightful short circuit from Comps.

In Comps, continue ahead for DRAGUIGNAN on the D955.

Just 1.8km south of Comps you pass a shrine and chapel off to the left — under five minutes' walk off the road — a lovely picnic spot with fine views left back to Comps and the valley of the Artuby (see photograph pages 144-145). Soon you enter a military zone dating from Julius Caesar's time on the **Plan de Canjuers**. Beyond the plateau the road winds downhill through pretty woodlands, where moss and ivy cling to the trees and stone walls. Ignore the road off left to the peach-coloured spread of **Montferrat**; keep right for DRAGUIGNAN on the D955.

Watch for the D54 left to Draguignan: ignore it but, just beyond it, fork right on the narrow D51 for CHATEAU-DOUBLE, AMPUS.

This beautifully-wooded road threads below high cliffs on the north side of the **river Nartuby**, through the pretty **Gorges de Châteaudouble**. A short tunnel takes you into the old village of **Châteaudouble**. Beyond here you enter the **Bois des Prannes**, a beautiful 5km-long stretch of mixed woodland. Oaks predominate, but there are sprinklings of Mediterranean pines. In spring the road is aglow with wild flowers.

Once out of the wood, a one-way system takes you below and to the left of **Ampus** (155km), where there is a well-restored Romanesque church with bell-cage.

Coming to a T-junction, ignore the right turn for 'Centre ville', go left for DRAGUIGNAN, TOURTOUR. After 250m, at a T-junction with the D49, go right for TOURTOUR. At the next junction, keep straight on for TOURTOUR (still D49). Then, when the D49 goes right to Verignon and the Gorges du Verdon, keep ahead for TOURTOUR (D51).

A pine wood takes you along to **St-Pierre-de-Tourtour**, a modern 'second-home' development. A roundabout with an ancient olive tree welcomes you to the hill village of **Tourtour**★ (163km *i✝⊞▓* ☞), where the 11th-century church of St-Denis stands well off to the left (photographs pages 146-147). Walk 30 begins in the main village square. The château now

houses the *mairie;* the tourist office is nearby. After wandering the lanes to admire the beautifully-restored old houses, walk to the church, from where there is a brilliant view★ stretching from the Gulf of St-Raphaël in the east to Mont Ventoux in the northwest, by way of the Montagne Ste-Victoire and the Lubéron.

Leave Tourtour from another roundabout with another ancient olive tree, taking the third exit (D51 for VILLECROZE).

Two kilometres outside Tourtour, look up right to spot the square **Tour de Grimaldi** (Walk 30) on a hill. Some 2km further on, you pass a path off left to a *table d'orientation.*

At a fork, ignore the road left for Villecroze; keep ahead on the D557 for AUPS. At the next junction keep right for AUPS.

Life centres round the plane-shaded square in **Aups** (176km *i✝⊞M*▓▓), with its 15th-century Gothic church, cafés and museum of modern art.

Clock-tower in Aups

Tour 8: GRAND CANYON DU VERDON

Aups • Moustiers-Ste-Marie • Grand Canyon du Verdon • Aiguines • Aups

162km/100mi; about 7-8h driving; Michelin map 340
Walks en route: 31, 32
A very early start is recommended: although the tour is short, you won't average more than 15km/h in the canyon if you stop at most of the viewpoints. If you plan to walk in the canyon, you should ideally spend the night at La Palud or the inn at Point Sublime, breaking the tour into two days. (If you will spend only one day in this area, it might be best to avoid Moustiers; you will lose too much time in this crowded tourist centre.) Be sure to fill up with petrol before leaving Aups! All the roads are good, and none is vertiginous. From November to March, however, you might find the corniche roads closed because of rock falls or, more rarely, snow. This landscape is the most visited natural wonder between the southern Alps and the Pyrenees; try to see it outside high summer, and avoid weekends. Note: The

banks of a river are defined with your back to the source; as the Verdon rises in the east, the rive droite (right bank) is to the north, and the rive gauche (left bank) to the south.

Picnic suggestions: The **Pont de Galetas** is our first, dramatic introduction to the Verdon at the mouth of the canyon. There is a large picnic site here (no tables), where you can rent a pedalo. A quieter place, where it's difficult to stop, is the **Maison Cantonnière de St-Maurin** (⊼), on grassy slopes overlooking the river. Another gorgeous setting is the confluence of the Verdon and Jabron at the **Clue de Carejuan** (busy on weekends and in high season). By contrast, no one makes the effort to descend to the Roman **Pont du Tusset** (photograph page 151), so you would have this gorgeous setting all to yourself if you do Short walk 32.

T he Grand Canyon du Verdon owes its name to the father of speleology, E-A Martel: 'We have here a real wonder, unique in Europe', he wrote; 'it is the most American of all the canyons in the Old World — and I've not changed my mind since seeing the Grand Canyon in Colorado'. It was Martel who first explored this 25km-long gorge, together with Isidore Blanc, a schoolteacher from Rougon. They set off on their three-day 'cruise' in August 1905 — in a rowing boat equipped with a wooden ladder and, it is said, dressed in overcoats and bowler hats (see also page 151). We urge you, too, to see the canyon from the river bed; its true grandeur can only be appreciated from the depths.

Leave Aups on the D957 north, following TOUTES DIRECTIONS at the roundabout where the photograph on page 49 was taken, then MOUSTIERS, LES SALLES at the next roundabout.

Just over 15km from Aups, pull out at the large parking area on the left (⌨) for a superb view ★ to the **Lac de Ste-Croix** and Les Salles. In the morning the sun shines on the burnt sienna cliffs ahead — a perfect backdrop for the glimmering turquoise lake and red roofs of **Les Salles**. Skirting the lake on the D957 (⌧ at 21km, 23km), you pass the D19 off right; this is the main westerly access road to the south bank of the canyon (the 'Corniche Sublime'). Keep straight ahead for *MOUSTIERS*.

As you cross the Verdon on the **Pont de Galetas** (25km), look right for a fantastic view★ into the milky-green waters of the gorge. Just over the bridge, you are in **Alpes de Haute-Provence**; pull up round the bend in the large parking area (⌧ with information panels; pedalo rentals), a perfect picnic setting beside the lake (but in summer and autumn beware: you may encounter a veritable cyclone of gnats and mosquitoes here). More good viewpoints are passed (⌧) before you climb away from the lake along the valley of the river **Maïre**.

At the roundabout, ignore the D952 right to Castellane *(or turn right here, if you are not going into Moustiers);* continue ahead to **Moustiers-Ste-Marie★** (32km *i*⌧**M**⌧).

Overspilling with day-trippers, Moustiers is best seen very early or late in the day. Its magnificent setting cannot be appreciated from this approach; you must park outside the village and walk in. A chain with a gold star is suspended between the cliffs dominating the village. High in a ravine, below the star, stands the 12/16th-century pilgrimage chapel of Notre-Dame-de-Beauvoir, from where there are fine views down over the rooftops of Moustiers and towards the Valensole Plateau. A wide walkway climbs to this chapel, past the 14 Stations of the Cross depicted in faïence. Moustiers grew rich on faïence during the 17th and 18th centuries and, while the industry declined in the 19th century, it has been revived today for the tourist trade. Unlike the tourist shops, the Musée de la Faïence contains only the finest examples of the art; it is next to the

The Verdon near the Clue de Chasteuil, with Robion in the background

Belvédère de l'Escalès (left) and the Tours des Trescaïres (above). Notice how the different layers of sediment are clearly seen in these twin pillars — as opposed to the smooth compact limestone of the Escalès climbing wall on the left.

Romanesque church with its impressive four-storey bell-tower.

From Moustiers return to the roundabout on the D952 passed earlier and go left towards CASTELLANE.

The road climbs steadily towards the north (right) bank of the canyon, soon entering the **Forêt Domaniale du Montdenier**; here and there you can pull up for views back over the lake (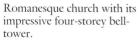). Watch out for the **Belvédère de Galetas★** (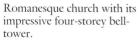), a large lay-by on the right 8km up from Moustiers *(not signposted)*. This is your last chance to look back over the lake and down to where the jade-green flow of the Verdon escapes from the narrow straits.

At this point you enter the **Grand Canyon du Verdon★** and follow the right bank to
52

the start of the canyon at the Clue de Carejuan. Throughout the tour the walls of the gorge will open and close like a bellows, in places narrowing down to only 200m/650ft across.

Just 1km beyond the Galetas viewpoint, you pass the old **Maison Cantonnière de St-Maurin** (⌂); the first abbey in Provence once stood on this site. Perhaps in an effort to stop the vandals (the building is covered in grafitti), a wooden barrier now bars the lay-by to cars. But it *is* possible to pull off the road a short way ahead if you want to picnic here — it's a lovely spot overlooking the river. Some 3.5km further on, beyond the Mayreste farm, a large parking area alerts you to the **Belvédère de Mayreste**. The viewpoint★ (⌖) lies 300m/yds up from the road, to the right. From here you have a first good outlook upstream into the canyon. A farm selling Verdon honey is passed on the right

Trigance, a good base for exploring the Verdon. If you visit in autumn, you may have the unforgettable experience of seeing a transhumance *(see page 173) in the village lanes.*

2km further on. At the **Belvédère du Col d'Ayen**, 2km past the farm, you have to walk another 250m/yds to the viewpoint★ (📷), looking ahead to the deepest and narrowest part of the canyon, where the walls are under 10m/30ft apart at the base. The river is an incredible 535m/1750ft below you here.

Now the road has turned away from the gorge, and you pass a 'panoramic' hotel on the right with a snack bar *(buvette)*. Look ahead to the beautiful spread of fields around La Palud and the still-distant pyramid of Robion, the mountain shown on page 51.

An 18th-century castle rises above **La Palud-sur-Verdon** (51.5km ■▲▲), an ideal base for walkers, where you will find guides, taxis, maps and provisions.

From La Palud continue east on the D952 towards Castellane, then turn right on the D23.

The road rises through fields of lavender and then a wood, to the edge of the canyon. You're now on the **Route des Crêtes★** — a 22km-long one-

way corniche road with no less than 16 superb viewpoints (📷); all have ample parking, but not all are signposted. Our favourites are highlighted below (see map pages 150-151).

The **Trescaïres** belvedere offers your first good view upstream towards the Samson Corridor and the inn at Point Sublime, with Rougon above it. Below you are the twin turrets shown on page 52 (right), the 'Tours des Trescaïres'. From the **Belvédère de l'Escalès** the view plunges down over a magnificent climbing wall rising 500m/1650ft above the river. The **Dent d'Aire** (🗻) boasts the only 360° viewpoint on this road. At the **Tilleul** viewpoint, a dizzying 565m/1850ft above the river, you are just opposite the gash of the Artuby gorge and not far south of the Escalès climbing wall and the honey-coloured cliffs of the Dent d'Aire. You're unlikely to miss the **Gorge de Guègues** (photograph page 2), where goats loll about on the concrete 'casting couch'. These film

53

extras will add scale to your photographs of the Plan de Canjuers in the southwest and Mt Robion in the east. From the **Belvédère des Glacières** there is a fine view to La Mescla (photograph below), where the Artuby flows into the Verdon, and the spine of rock enclosed in the meander of the Verdon.

The **Belvédère de Guègues**, on a tight hairpin bend, looks back to La Mescla and over right to a narrow corridor of rock called the 'Cavaliers'. Not much further along, you come to the **Chalet de la Maline**, from where Walk 31 descends to the Sentier Martel — the most popular footpath in the canyon. Just past the chalet, you catch the Verdon in one of its more tranquil moods, at the **Estellié Belvedere**. Finally, the belvederes of **L'Imbut** and **Maugué** offer exceptionally good plunging views into the gorge (now 'only' 300m/ 1000ft below you), but nothing is to be seen of the river itself — it's buried under a chaos of rock. Soon the road runs through a Swiss-Alpine landscape of rolling fields, and you come back to **La Palud** (76km).

Again head west on the D952 *for* CASTELLANE.

Away from the drama of the canyon, there is a fine view left into the **Baou Valley**, its emerald fields dotted with solitary farmsteads. Almost opposite the road up left to Rougon, pull over right at the **Point Sublime** (83km 🏔 ✖),

the three-star viewpoint on the north bank. *After locking everything in the boot of your car,* follow signposting to the railed viewpoint★ (📷 15min return) above the confluence of the Baou and Verdon. Before you is the magnificent cleft of the Samson Corridor. Why not spend the night at the inn here, to enjoy this superb setting to the full? In the morning you can watch the mists rise over the canyon and then set out on Walk 31 or Walk 32. At the very least, *do* try to get down to the Pont du Tusset (Short walk 32; photograph page 153) or the Baume aux Pigeons (Short walk 31).

Continue ahead from the Point Sublime *for 0.7km and then, just before a tunnel, turn very sharp right on the* D23a.

This road takes you down *into* the **Samson Corridor★**, where it ends at a large parking

From the Balcons de la Mescla, you look down on the confluence of the Verdon and Artuby 250m/800ft below.

area — just where the river **Bau** flows into the Verdon (photograph page 152). Walk 31 comes in here, after following the Sentier Martel from below the Chalet de la Maline, and Short walk 31 to the Baume aux Pigeons begins here. This is the easiest access to the gorge for walkers, which is why it is usually so *very* crowded (another good reason to spend the night at the inn and jump the queue!).

Return to the main road and turn right through the short tunnel.

Now the balcony road begins its descent towards the river. At the **Clue de Carejuan**, the entrance to the canyon, beautifully-coloured strata arc over the road, and the river surges by on the right. There is parking here on the right, for a picnic area across the **Pont de Carejuan**, a gorgeous setting at the confluence of the Verdon and **Jabron** rivers. You're heading straight towards the escarpment of **Robion**.

Turn sharp right on the D955 for COMPS.

You cross the Verdon on the **Pont de Soleils**. (Tour 7 explores the Verdon further east, between here and Castellane; Tour 5 follows it north towards its source above Allos.) Go through the delightful honey-coloured hamlet of **Soleils**, bright with seasonal blooms. Then round a bend to enjoy a first view★ of **Trigance** (✕).

Take the D90 right towards the village; then, at the T-junction, turn left (still D90).

You pass to the left of Trigance (the photograph on page 53 was taken here).

At the D71 turn right.

At the **Col de St-Maimes** (☞), there is another fine view to Trigance, Robion and heights west of Castellane. Here we begin our tour of the south bank (*rive gauche*), the **Corniche Sublime★** (not to be confused with the Point Sublime on the north bank). The twin **Balcons de la Mescla★** (109km ☞ ✹) are two of the best lookout points in the canyon. From here the view plunges straight down 250m/800ft to the confluence of the Verdon and **Artuby** rivers, at a point where the Verdon describes a very tight meander around a knife-edge of rock (photograph pages 54-55). The Mescla ('mixture' in Provençal) is one of the most beautiful stages on the Sentier Martel, where the pebbly shores of the river are an ideal picnic spot. You can see the footpath on the north bank, running below the Route des Crêtes.

Pull away from the Verdon once again, this time above the sheer walls of the Artuby ravine, which is soon crossed on the **Pont de l'Artuby★**. This bridge is astoundingly beautiful for a modern (1947) concrete structure; it spans the river with a single arch. Pull up just before (☞) or after (☞ and seasonal ✹) crossing, to admire not only the bridge, but the spectacular view into the very narrow Artuby gorge. As you enter the **Réserve Géologique de Haute-Provence**, the road skirts the edge of the canyon but, unfortunately, trees and a roadside barrier prevent stopping along this stretch. (For much of the way this corniche road does *not* hug the cliff-edge; you remain at some distance from the gorge and keep making forays to the viewpoints.)

The **Belvédère d'Avelan** (☞ via a path off left and then right, 400m in all) offers a good view of the Artuby and the juncture of the two canyons. *Alert:* When you approach the **Tunnels de Fayet**, *be prepared to pull over right into the single-space lay-by* just beyond the first tunnel★ (☞)! This is one of the finest viewpoints on the tour, from where you can see the great cradle of the canyon, with the river flowing in from the northeast and downstream to the northwest. Beyond the second tunnel (entered immediately), the river widens out and the views are not as fine. Then you head inland across moorland and gentle rolling hills, the most northerly reach of the **Plan de Canjuers**. Park just before **Les Cavaliers★** (114km ▲ ✕ ☞): from the terrace of the restaurant the views take in the canyon upstream and down, but what most impresses are the 300m/ 1000ft-high sheer cliffs below and the proximity to the north bank (legend had it that horsemen could jump from one wall to the other in a single leap, hence the name). Just beyond here, there is a similar outlook from the **Estellié** belvedere (☞), from where you can see the path descending from the Chalet de la Maline to the Sentier Martel. From here the road skirts the edge of the canyon for some 3km — one of the most impressive parts of the tour, with fine views both upstream and down, but with few parking places. It's worth leaving the car at one of the lay-bys and walking along the road for a short time. As you

Château and church at Aiguines. There is a museum here devoted to the old craft of wood turning, which once gave employment to most of the inhabitants. Box was used to make these beautiful objects, because of its hard wood, colour and delicate graining. In the depths of the canyon, protected by the cliffs, the shrub grew to perhaps 10m/30ft high, sometimes with trunks up to 20cm/8in in diameter. Gathering these prize specimens was dangerous work. The box-cutters were veritable goats, descending hair-raising paths into the depths (or in some cases abseiling down with ropes); they then lived in caves by the river's edge for months at a time. The cut trees were floated down-river to where they were taken by mule to Aiguines.

look upstream from the **Falaise de Baucher★** (📷), the Verdon races through the steep narrow defile, where it soon disappears under boulders at a rock chaos 400m/1300ft below the **Pas de l'Imbut** (📷).

From the **Margés** viewpoint★ (📷) you look upstream to the tail of the lake and the end of the canyon, with the Valensole Plateau rising in the west. Then the road turns away from the gorge in a wide arc, the **Cirque de Vaumale**. At the **Source de Vaumale★** (📷) there are magnificent views to the west — as far as the Lubéron and Mont Ventoux — and north over the viewpoints on the Route des Crètes. The Mayreste farm, where the Verdon disgorges into the lake, is seen below on the north bank. The river is more than 700m/2300ft below you here. This is the highest part of the south bank road and, at 1200m/4000ft, it's almost like flying over the spectacle in a helicopter. The helicopter landing pad at the **Col d'Illoire** (📷) brings you back down to earth: here you finally leave the canyon. Enjoy a last look at the rock walls, but you will not see the river again. See if you can spot the Montagne Ste-Victoire in the west from here.

As you descend towards Aiguines there is an excellent long view (📷) towards the **Valensole Plateau** across the lake; in autumn its fields are a wash of russets and golds. Soon the multi-coloured glazed tiles decorating the four towers of the 17th-century château at **Aiguines** (134km ▥M🏛) glisten in the sun, immediately drawing your attention to its proud setting above the lake, with the church beside it on the left (📷 with *table d'orientation*).

Having joined the D19 on the approach to the village, follow it through Aiguines and past a viewpoint out to the Lac de Ste-Croix (📷🍴).

Some 3km from Aiguines, turn left on the D71 for TAVERNES. When you come to the D957 turn left for LES SALLES, AUPS. Then follow this road all the way back to **Aups** *(162km).*

You pass an attractive war memorial in the form of a broken Greek column. On the left the strata of the Plain de Canjuers glisten in the low sun.

Tour 9: THE MAURES

Aups • Lorgues • Vidauban • La Garde-Freinet • La Croix-Valmer • Chartreuse de la Verne • Notre-Dame-des-Anges • Collobrières • Besse-sur-Issole • Carcès • Aups

243km/151mi; about 7-8h driving; Michelin map 340

Walks en route: 33, (34)

Because of the danger of forest fires, many of the roads in the Maures are closed to the public. This tour uses the only east/west road open to motor vehicles — the D14 on the middle ridge. Be prepared for very slow motoring in the Maures and on the St-Tropez Peninsula; roads are narrow and winding. The tour does not take in the famed Corniche des Maures (D559) because for much of the year it is a misery of traffic. If you come outside high season and can spend an extra day, do consider driving the stretch from La Croix-Valmer to

Bormes-les-Mimosas and Le Lavandou.

Picnic suggestions: The **D48** and **D558** at the start of the Maures circuit offer lovely picnicking under cork oaks or umbrella pines; one of the most picturesque settings is a bridge crossed at the junction of these two roads. There are also pleasant places to pull over on the **D14**, with views over the Périer Valley. If you were to detour to **Gigaro** (just before La Croix-Valmer), you could follow Short walk 34 and picnic under shady umbrella pines after about 15 minutes' walking (photograph page 160).

Apart from the great beauty of its forests of oak, pine and chestnut, the Maures massif is fascinating for reasons both geological and historical. These are among the oldest mountains in France, part of a great continent existing during the Primary Era, some 500 million years ago. Today that continent lies below the Mediterranean, and all that remains of this crystalline land mass are the Maures and Esterel, and the islands of Corsica, Sardinia and the Balearics (as well as the Lérins, just off the coast). More recent history saw the massif as the first staging post in the invasion of southern France on 15 August 1944, when Allied forces landed between Hyères and St-Raphaël (see Walk 7). The French pushed west to Marseille and the Americans north to Grenoble and east to Nice; Provence was liberated in 15 days. For two massifs rising almost side by side, the Maures and Esterel could not be more different: where the Esterel is a jagged upthrust of red, the Maures present a more comfortable landscape of rolling fir-green ridges.

From Aups follow VILLECROZE, DRAGUIGNAN, heading south past the petrol station on the D557. After 0.5km fork left for VILLECROZE (still D557).

Watch for the sign denoting the entrance to **Villecroze** and, 0.3km beyond it, pull over left into the municipal park, where a signposted path leads past a

The mairie at Lorgues — just one of the beautiful façades flanking the plane-shaded square

lovely high waterfall to some intriguing 16th-century cave dwellings (small charge for a guided tour). Continue beside the ivy-creepered walls of Villecroze and keep ahead for FLAYOSC, DRAGUIGNAN on the D557. Crossing a river, you pass two extensive *domaines*.

At the roundabout where the D560 comes in from Salernes, go left on the D557 for FLAYOSC, DRAGUIGNAN, LORGUES; then, 1.5km further on, go right on the D10 for LORGUES. Meeting the Lorgues ring road at a roundabout, follow CENTRE VILLE (third exit). There's a one-way system in the centre and no signposting (at press date): we suggest you park as soon as you see the marie shown above.

Lorgues ★ (22km *i*✝⚄) is worth a break: stroll along the plane-shaded square (one of the finest in the region) and into the pedestrian precinct; be sure to see the 18th-century church of St-Martin and the 14th-century walls.

To leave Lorgues, turn back from the mairie and go left in front of the pharmacy. Coming down to a roundabout on the ring road, take the fifth exit (D562: LE MUY, DRAGUIGNAN).

Now you have a lovely view left back to Lorgues, focussing on the church with its square bell tower and impressive buttresses.

At the next roundabout take the first exit, the D10 for VIDAUBAN.

The road heads towards the sweet little chapel of **Ste-Anne**.

After 3.5km bear right on the D48 for VIDAUBAN.

You descend through the oaks of the **Bois d'Astros** and pass the magnificent **Château d'Astros** on the right, surrounded by its vineyards and orchards; it once belonged to the Knights of Malta. After crossing the river **Argens**, you come into **Vidauban** (34km *i*), an ancient town which once traded in silkworm moths' eggs.

Turn right in front of the pedestrian precinct, then take the second left, to leave Vidauban on the D48 for LA GARDE-FREINET.

The road passes under the railway and then the motorway. The landscape alternates between chartreuse-green vineyards and lovely stands of umbrella pines, with fine places to stop. The snakeskin-like trunks of these trees are fascinating, with their black and white diamond patterning. Note, but ignore, the D74 left to Plan-de-la-Tour: 2.5km further on you cross a bridge. This is one of the prettiest picnic settings, with a choice of umbrella pines or the river's edge.

Just over the bridge turn left for LA GARDE-FREINET on the D558. This lovely road through cork oaks, umbrella pines, and vineyards is usually *very* busy. We like to drive it on Sundays at lunch time, when it's virtually empty! Now the most northerly and highest range in the Maures rears up ahead. When the younger 'upstarts', the Pyrenees and the Alps, emerged in the Tertiary Period a mere 50 million years ago, their upheavals reshaped the existing land mass, creating the three parallel east/west ridges that today make up the massif. Unfortunately, today only the middle ridge is open to traffic, due to the danger of forest fires.

The red-tiled roofs of **La Garde-Freinet** (53km *i* □ ♤) are dominated by a ruined Saracen fort.

Leave La Garde-Freinet by keeping on the D558 south for GRIMAUD (not signposted).

The road passes to the right of beautifully-kept **Grimaud**

Notre-Dame-des-Anges, dwarfed by the adjacent relay tower

(64km *i* ♣ □ ♤), with its impressive ruined castle (you will have a lovely view of the setting later in the tour).

Keep following COGOLIN, ST-TROPEZ through Grimaud (D558). Then, at the roundabout where the D558 goes right to Cogolin at the first exit, take the next exit, the D14 for ST-TROPEZ. Just under 1km further on, turn right on the D61 (also signposted to ST-TROPEZ). Keep straight over a roundabout (ST-TROPEZ).

The road runs through vineyards edged by golden grasses and you cross the river **Giscle**.

At the D98 roundabout, take the third exit (ST-TROPEZ). Now keep following green signs for ST-TROPEZ, joining the D98a. Ramatuelle is also signed below St-Tropez (white signs).*

Continue straight past Luna Park on your right.

Just over 2km from joining the D98, turn off right on the D61 for GASSIN and RAMATUELLE, leaving the D98a for St-Tropez off to the left.

As soon as you turn off, the village of Gassin rises straight ahead. Like La Garde-Freinet and Grimaud, Gassin was perched high enough to spot a sea-borne invader and far enough inland from the coast to enable the inhabitants to take defensive action.

Just over 1km along turn right for GASSIN on the C1.

Or, to shorten the tour and avoid getting stuck in a traffic jam on the St-Tropez Peninsula, take the first exit for HYERES, TOULON and pick up the tour just past the 103km-point.

Cork oaks near La Garde-Freinet. Cork oaks flourish on the silica-rich soils of the Maures and Esterel, and they are assiduously cultivated for industrial use; most of the bark stripped from these trees will make bottle-corks.

The road climbs from flat vineyards into trees and past the substantial vineyards of Château Minuty on the left. You also bypass the centre of **Gassin**, forking left outside the village and leaving it off to your right, above grassy terraces.

Now watch for small white signposts and, at a Y-fork just outside Gassin, go right for RAMATUELLE, LA CROIX VALMER. At the next Y-fork go left for RAMATUELLE (where a right is signposted to La Croix-Valmer).

After rising over the **Col de Paillas**, turn up left to park at the ruined **Moulins de Paillas**. From here you can find vantage points between the trees for a view (📷) over the vineyards of the peninsula and out to the azure sea.

From the windmills continue towards Ramatuelle.

Ramatuelle (82km ✝🎔🎔) is a pink and honey-coloured village set above vineyards, with a 17th-century Romanesque church. The one-way system takes you to the right of the church and centre.

Leaving the village, first follow TOUTES DIRECTIONS (D61) and then, at a roundabout, take the first exit for LA CROIX-VALMER (D93).

Climbing through umbrella pines, you enjoy a lovely view westwards as you crest the **Col de Collebasse**. Some 2km further on, from the **Hauts de Gigaro**, you look down left over the setting for Walk 34 — the beautiful stretch of coast shown on page 160.* The road continues to a roundabout on the D559 at **La Croix-Valmer** (96km *i*🎔🎔).

Take the first exit for GASSIN, COGOLIN (D559). Follow this road through a major junction with the D98/D98a (you've been here earlier in the tour). Watch for green signs at the far end of the junction and turn left for HYERES and TOULON on the D98 (103km). Follow this road to a roundabout just outside Cogolin, then take the first exit for GRIMAUD and COGOLIN CENTRE (D558).

Busy **Cogolin** (107km *i*) can be a nightmare to get through; follow GRIMAUD at all forks.

On the edge of town, just past the Lidl supermarket on the left, you come to another roundabout: take the third exit here, the D48 for COLLOBRIERES.

---

*If you are going to Walk 34, watch carefully for a left turn to GIGARO a little over 2.5km further on, and from there keep following GIGARO down to the coast. Park along the esplanade, just before the road turns inland.

Pull over right at the edge of the hamlet of St-Maur (where the church has a sweet tiny bell-cage), for a superb view across vineyards towards the twin towers of the ruined castle at Grimaud.

Turn left on the D14 for COLLO-BRIERES.

As you head up the middle ridge of the massif (the only ridge now open to motor traffic), the grass- and heather-lined road is beautiful from the outset, framed by cork oaks and rolling vineyards dotted with farms (). The deep Périer Valley opens up on the left, cloaked in a thick mantle of almost-black trees. ('Maures' is derived from the Provençal *mauro*, a word applied to dark woodlands.) Soon you notice the reservoir below (Barrage de la Verne; photograph pages 156-157), and the buildings on the far side of the valley — the

Chartreuse de la Verne (), setting for Walk 33. Beyond the **Col de Taillude**, where you feel really deep in these velvety, oak-clad mountains, turn left on the D214 (a very narrow road but with adequate passing places) to the **Chartreuse de la Verne** (132km ♱), a Carthusian monastery dating from the 12th century (open 11.00-18.00 in summer, 10.00-17.00 in winter; closed Christmas, Easter, Ascension, 5 August and 1 November). After your visit *do* follow Walk 33 for 10 minutes or so, to enjoy some superb views.

Return to the D14 and turn left.

Soon the typically complex relay station atop Notre-Dame-des-Anges looms over the landscape like a hovering spacecraft.

Some 3km short of Collobrières, turn right on the D39.

The heavily-wooded road winds uphill towards the Col des Fourches, with brief glimpses towards La Sauvette on the right — the highest peak in the massif (and Var), at 779m/2555ft.

Just before the pass, turn left for NOTRE-DAME-DES-ANGES.

The old priory of **Notre-Dame-des-Anges**, remodelled in the 19th century, is rather dwarfed by the huge relay nearby. Through breaks in the trees, there are some fine views north towards the Alps and south over the Maures to the sea.

Leave Notre-Dame the way you came but, instead of returning to the D39, head south on the forestry road (DFC1) down the **Vallon des Vaudrèches**. *Back at the D14, turn right.*

Sweet chestnut trees surround **Collobrières** (168km 🕰), a market town specialising in chestnut delicacies, especially *marrons glacés*. The shaded square is one of our favourites in the south of France and an enchanting place to stop for a break; one of the cafés on the north side of the square has a terrace overlooking the fast-flowing river behind the houses.

Leave Collobrières on the D14 for CUERS, TOULON.

This road runs through the wide **Réal Collobrier Valley**, with far-reaching vistas of gently-rolling vineyards against a backdrop of dark green trees.

About 10km from Collobrières, 2km short of Pierrefeu turn right at a small blue sign on the right: DFC1, CHEMIN DE MARAVAL (very easily missed).

You pass through vineyards and orchards, cross the Réal Collobrier and then go through the hamlet of **La Tuilière**.

Just outside La Tuilière, fork left for HAMEAU DES DAVIDS (sign: ROUTE DU VALLON DE MARAVAL.) At a T-junction, turn left for HAMEAU DES VIDAUX. After crossing the Réal Martin, turn right on the D13 for CARNOULES and PIGNANS.

Now the oak-clad lower slopes of the Maures give way to the vineyards of the **Réal Martin Valley** down on your right, protected by cane windbreaks and dotted with fruit trees.

Some 3.5km along, at a Y-fork, go left on the D13 for CARNOULES. Drive under the motorway, then keep right for

Restful pastel façades and shady plane trees characterise the beautiful main square at Collobrières.

Typical Maures scenery — this pretty setting for a picnic is on the D14, near the junction with the D48.

CARNOULES. *At **Carnoules** (191km) go under the railway and turn left on the D97, then go right for BESSE-S/ISSOLE and CARCES (D13). Follow CARCES, BESSE through the narrow streets, to leave Carnoules on the D13.*

Beyond a beautiful *domaine* on the right, the flat stretch of road is punctuated by cypress spires and wind-bent planes.

At the roundabout before BESSE, take the first exit for FLASSANS (D13). Keep following FLASSANS, but ignore the D13a off right into the centre. Cross straight over the DN7 towards CABASSE/ABBAYE DU THORONET.

The DN7 was the old Via Aurelia linking Italy with Arles. The D13 runs under the motorway and straight through **Cabasse**.

At the T-junction past Cabasse, turn left for CARCES, still on the D13. (A right would take you to the Abbaye du Thoronet, a detour of 8km return.)

(The 12th-century Abbaye du Thoronet is 'sister' to the Cistercian abbeys of Sénanque and Silvacane visited in

Landscapes of western Provence during Car tour 2.)

Soon the **Lac de Carcès** sparkles on the left; you skirt its banks for 4km to **Carcès** (⚐⚑), where the **Gros Bessillon** rises in the northwest.

Follow COTIGNAC from Carcès, to keep on the D13.

The road crosses the **Argens River**, then the river **Cassole**, immediately beyond which the D13 turns 90° right. Entering **Cotignac** (⚐⚑), keep right (where 'Centre ville' is left). The D13 circles to the right of the centre. Climbing above Cotignac you pass to the right of the two ruined towers of the Château de Castellane.

Turn right on the D22 for AUPS. After 5km turn right for SALERNS, AUPS on the D560.

Sillans-la-Cascade is a lovely small touristic village.

At Sillans fork left for AUPS on the D22.

Soon a straight stretch of road affords brilliant views ahead, to the golden walls of the Grand Canyon du Verdon.

*At a roundabout, take the third exit, back to **Aups** (243km).*

Tour 10: LA MONTAGNE STE-VICTOIRE

Aups • Lac de Ste-Croix • Tavernes • Rians • Barrage de Bimont • Pourrières • Le Tholonet • Aix-en-Provence

164km/102mi; about 5h driving; Michelin map 340
Walks en route: 35, 36
The tour follows good, if sometimes winding, roads. The road over the Montagne des Ubacs is very narrow, but not vertiginous. Fill up with petrol at Aups or Rians.

Picnic suggestions: Beyond Jouques you pass the gorgeous honey-coloured farm of **Gerle** on the left. Just before it comes into view, you could park and picnic in the shade of pines (rocks to sit on). Sadly, there is no parking just a little further on where, in spring, the most fantastic poppy fields you are ever likely to see will be in bloom. The **Barrage de Bimont**, a huge man-made lake, is ideal for picnicking (but can be very busy on weekends and in high season). The **Col des Portes** (⌂) on the north side of the Montagne Ste-Victoire is an impressive setting, full of wild flowers. On the south side of the mountain, there are parking places under pines all the way along the **Route Cézanne** (photographs pages 4-5, 70 and 162-163). For something intriguingly different, a really shady grotto for a hot day, park at **Le Tholonet** and follow Walk 36 for 25 minutes, to the ford by the watercourse, where you can perch atop the stumpy concrete pillars (photograph page 166).

O f all the painters and subjects associated with the south of France, Paul Cézanne's daunting struggle to capture the essence of the Montagne Ste-Victoire comes first to mind. Cézanne was born in Aix-en-Provence and, although his father wanted him to study law, he was drawn to the arts. He interrupted his studies to join Emile Zola, an old friend from school days, in Paris. There Zola introduced him to some of the leading Impressionists, who inspired his early work. But he never felt 'at home' in Paris, nor with the Impressionist School. He returned to Aix and developed his own style, crafting luminous geometric planes to express form — a precursor of Cubism. The Montagne Ste-Victoire became an obsessive subject, and he painted it more than 50 times. You can visit Cézanne's *atelier* in Aix (Avenue Paul Cézanne), and the Musée Granet, which has a gallery devoted to his pictures.

Leave Aups by heading north on the D957 via roundabouts (first TOUTES DIRECTIONS, then LES SALLES, MOUSTIERS. Some 7.5km from Aups, take the D49 left for BAUDUEN.

All at once you come upon the magnificent view★ shown on page 66 (☞), over the turquoise-green Lac de Ste-Croix. Bauduen is seen ahead on the lake, an attractive cluster of red roof-tiles; behind it is Les Salles and to the west the perched village of Ste-Croix. *Don't continue to Bauduen;*

The Lac de Ste-Croix and Bauduen, from the D49

turn left on the D71 for RIEZ.

Now skirting the **Lac de Ste-Croix★** (📷), you'll spot the little *belvédère* atop Notre-Dame-de-Baudinard on the hill to the left, by a farmhouse.

When the road forks, don't cross the dam to round the lake; keep left on the D71. (Or, if you don't plan to do any walking today, you could cross the dam here and take the 'Circuit touristique du lac', going via Moustiers-Ste-Marie and the D957, rejoining the tour at this point; add 58km.)

After 2km your road joins the D9: continue ahead, ignoring the road off right to Riez. As you climb away from the lake, swathes of lavender fields run off the road; you're at the heart of the 'Route de la Lavande', which extends west to Sault (see *Landscapes of western Provence*, Car tour 3). The road squeezes through the narrow lanes of **Baudinard-sur-Verdon**, a pretty village.

At the fork outside Baudinard keep right for MONTMEYAN, again on the D71.

You may be surprised — since you're in France, not Texas — to pass large breeding stables for horses in a setting which would not have been out of place in the old classic TV 'soap' *Dallas*; we call it 'South-fork'. Attractively cultivated fields take you to a T-junction 3km beyond the ranch: turn left here for MONTMEYAN. Now the road is straight for about 7km, and there may be military vehicles about; like the Plan de Canjuers, this area is used for army manoeuvres. After you cross the D271, golden cereal crops embroidered with wild flowers edge both sides of the road, a pleasant change from a surfeit of vineyards or lavender.

When you come to a T-junction with the D30, turn right for MONTMEYAN. Just outside **Montmeyan***, at a T-junction with the D13, turn left for TAVERNES, BARJOLS; but, only 400m further on, at a round-about, take the third exit, the D13 for TAVERNES, BARJOLS.*

You pass the pink, turreted château of **L'Eouvière** with

glazed roof-tiles off to the right of the road.

When the D13 goes left for Carcès, keep right on the D71 for TAVERNES.

After 3.5km you pass the **Château de la Curnière** *domaine* on the left. Head straight through **Tavernes** (45.5km ♟), where an exquisite bell-cage rises atop the church tower.

At the junction past the church (off to the right) go right on the D554 for RIANS.

Leaving Tavernes you cross a flat agricultural plain, with good views to the twin Bessillon peaks in the southeast. At **Varages** (53km ♟) the Romanesque church has a multi-coloured glazed tile roof.

Keep following ESPARRON, RIANS, to leave Varages on the D561 west.

Approaching **St-Martin**, its château rises on a wooded hill on the left. In **Esparron** (⚖) keep straight on for RIANS, passing the faded-rose façade of the old wine cooperative on the left — a lovely focal point for a photograph. Just outside Esparron, stop at the cemetery chapel of **Notre-Dame** on the left, covered with ivy and flanked by cypresses. Straight ahead is the **Montagne d'Artigues**, a conical hill. Mixed cultivation backed by gentle hills takes you to **Rians** (*i*✖🛒⚖).

The D561 passes to the right of the centre. Follow JOUQUES at all the roundabouts, to leave Rians on the D561 west. The service station at the third roundabout is your last chance for petrol for some 80km.

The Canal de Provence is now on your right. After crossing the canal you pass a gorgeous rose-tinted farm on the right, the **Mas St-Maurin**, fronted by a double avenue of planes and backed by the Montagne de Vautubière. Rounding a bend, you will be taken completely by surprise to find yourself in a tiny gorge, where you drive under a suspension bridge carrying the massive pipe of the Canal de Provence

Whimsical bell-cage at Tavernes and pipe carrying the Canal de Provence, west of Rians

across the valley into **Bouches-du-Rhône**.

*Just as you approach **Jouques**, go left on the D11 for VAUVENARGUES, SAMBUC. At a Y-fork, keep left on the D11.*

The road passes the cypress-studded chapel of **St-Antonin** on the right and a canal control centre. Now you see another gorgeous farm — **Gerle**, a cluster of honeyed stone on the left. Just before it comes fully into view, there is a pleasant pine-shaded picnic place with rocks to sit on. Another bend, and another surprise — in spring: you look down left over a scarlet sea of poppies★. Then the narrow wooded road climbs the **Montagne des Ubacs**.

On cresting a rise, the northern flanks of the **Montagne Ste-Victoire★** spread out in front of you — a brilliant sight. A shallow gorge takes you down through *garrigues;* while the river, on your left, is bone-dry, in spring this is a delightful run, when the pale new shoots on the holm oaks glitter like olive leaves against the older, dark green foliage.

On meeting the D10 (96km), turn right.

You pass above **Vauvenargues** (■ and *i* for Sainte-Victoire). There is ample parking on this main road (🖼), from where you can photograph the 14/17th-century château below in the village, where Picasso lived from 1958 until his death — and where he is buried. This road is also a good viewpoint towards the cross atop Ste-Victoire. Now, if you are doing Walk 35, *watch for your parking place,* 2km after passing above the château: pull over left to a bus stop and car park

with information boards and a large sign (among others): 'PRIEURE DE SAINTE-VICTOIRE'. This is **Les Cabassols**, from where the GR9 climbs the mountain.

Continuing west, soon Ste-Victoire disappears from view, but the road is edged with attractive fields.

Some 4.5km from Les Cabassols, turn sharp left on the D10f for BARRAGE DE BIMONT (not well signposted; opposite a sign for L'Oustau de St Marc).

Through the pines you have a splendid view of the mountain and cross. There is a large parking area at the **Barrage de Bimont★** (106km; crowded Sundays/holidays). This huge reservoir, fed by the Canal de Provence, provides water for 22 communities around Aix and even supplements the supplies to Marseille. From the 100m/330ft-high dam there is a path to the summit of Ste-Victoire and a track to the Barrage Zola (Alternative walk 36-2); see map and photographs on pages 166-167.

Leave the dam and turn right on the D10.

As you retrace your route on the north side of Ste-Victoire, you will have a fine view of its rippling flanks for the next 10 kilometres. Beyond Vauvenargues and the D11 from the Montagne des Ubacs, you cross the **Col des Claps** and pass below **La Citadelle** on the left, with its bright white limestone edge. Now the **Pic des Mouches** (1011m/3320ft), the highest summit on Ste-Victoire, rises on the right; beyond it, the mountain starts to tail off.

There is limited parking at the

The beautiful 18th-century château at Le Tholonet houses the offices of the Canal de Provence. This 220km-long watercourse, drawn principally from the Durance, has a total catchment network of 3000km and irrigates 115 communities in Bouches-du-Rhône and Var. Walk 36 would take you to an intriguing little gorge behind the château.

Col des Portes (120.5km 📷), from where a path climbs to a *table d'orientation* on the Pic des Mouches. This is also a pleasant picnic area (🍴 a few hundred metres beyond the col), especially in spring, when blue grass lilies *(Aphyllanthes monspeliensis)* and white-flowering Montpellier *Cistus* bloom under the holly and holm oaks — but there is no view to Ste-Victoire from here. Entering Var, the road is numbered D223.

At a junction outside Le-Puits-de-Rians go right on the D23 for POURRIERES.

Notice the slender, graceful trunks of the oaks here in the **Bois de Pourrières**. Some 4km along, limestone again makes its presence felt, bordering the road; then you round a bend and a fantastic edge rises before you — **Mont Aurélien** in the south, Ste-Victoire's little brother.

Pity the poor village of **Pourrières** (135.5km 🏘): its name signifies 'putrid' and supposedly recalls rotting corpses left on a battlefield here in 100BC.

Leave Pourrières on the D623 for PUYLOUBIER.

You travel across the plain shown on pages 4-5, where Ste-Victoire rises above a carpet of vineyards. This is a lovely run late in the afternoon, when the low sun highlights every nuance in the mountain's limestone ribs.

On crossing into **Bouches-du-Rhône** again, you come into **Puyloubier**, where the rose-coloured church with wrought-iron bell-cage sits nicely above the village.

From Puyloubier head west on the D17 for LE THOLONET.

Now on the **Route Cézanne★**, you skirt the southern foothills of Ste-Victoire, a blaze of yellow-

and blue-flowering blooms in spring. There are many pine-shaded parking places on this side of the mountain; all make fine picnic spots. The road passes to the right of **St-Antonin**, skirting the mountain in the setting shown on pages 162-163 (bottom). After you pass beneath the cross on Ste-Victoire (Croix de Provence), you curve downhill in hairpins. There are several routes up the mountain from this side, but they are all tougher than the ascents from the north.

On coming to **Le Tholonet** (158km), there is ample parking in front of the château shown on page 69 or in the plane-shaded square opposite. Walk 36 starts here and visits a pretty little reservoir southwest of the Lac de Bimont; engineered by Emile Zola's father 100 years before its post-war neighbour, it boasted the first arch dam in the world.

From Le Tholonet keep straight ahead on the D17, winding through pines and past impressive estates with wrought-iron gates. This road takes you straight into **Aix-en-Provence** (164km ✝✗M♺). Plan to spend a couple of days in this beautiful city, to visit the museums and spend the evenings strolling from fountain to fountain along the magnificent Cours Mirabeau, beneath the vaulting of plane trees. Then join the university students for an *apéritif* at one of the many outdoor cafés facing the elegant 17/18th-century mansions.

One morning, head back east on the Route Cézanne to see the mountain in early light. Go past Le Tholonet and turn right on the D46 to **Beaurecueil** (*i* for Sainte-Victoire), from where you will have the splendid view shown below.

The Montagne Ste-Victoire from the D46 to Beaurecueil. The village is home to the southerly information headquarters for the mountain; the northerly information centre is in Vauvenargues.

Walking

Those who go to France purely for a walking holiday are likely to be tackling the long linear GR routes. *This book has been written for motorists who want to tour some of the most beautiful roads in eastern Provence and enjoy one or two walks en route.* Very few of the walks are strenuous — we don't include hikes to summits that can be reached by car (like Utelle). The walks have been chosen to highlight the great variety of landscapes in this part of Provence and to focus on our favourite beauty spots.

Although the walks are scattered between the Alps and Aix, you should find many within easy reach (no more than an hour away by car or public transport) wherever you are based. If you are staying in one area for a couple of weeks, buy the relevant IGN 'Top 25' map (see page 7) and visit the nearest tourist office to ask about local walks and up-to-date **bus/train timetables** (many walks are accessible by public transport; see 'How to get there' at the top of each walk).

Weather
Many walks in this book can be done year round, but from mid-June to mid-September it will be far too hot to enjoy any but the easiest rambles. *Moreover, trails in forestry areas (the Esterel, Maures and Ste-Victoire for example) may be closed from 21 June to 30 September if the fire risk is high: check the map, updated daily, at www.paca.gouv.fr/files.massif).* Spring and autumn are the best seasons for walking; not only are the temperatures moderate, but there is an extravaganza of wild flowers and seasonal foliage. On the other hand, you will have to put up with a few days of torrential rain. In winter the walks in the Mercantour will be 'off bounds' *(some access roads may even be closed between mid-October and mid-June)*, and it may be *bitterly* cold atop Ste-Victoire or in the Verdon, even if there is no snow. *Always take local advice before walking in the high mountains between October and May.* The notorious *mistral* blows for about a third of the year (usually in winter/spring and usually for a *minimum* of three days). It can be difficult to stand upright, and no walks should be attempted in areas exposed to this northerly wind.

What to take

No special equipment is needed for any of the walks, but proper **walking boots** are preferable to any other footwear. Most walks in Provence cross very stony terrain at some stage, and good ankle support is essential. In wet weather you will also be glad of the waterproofing. A **sunhat** and high-protection **suncream** are equally important; there is a real risk of sunstroke on some walks. *All year round* it is advisable to carry a first-aid kit, whistle, smartphone (the emergency number throughout Europe is 112), torch, spare socks and bootlaces, and some warm clothing (the *mistral* can blow up suddenly, with temperatures dropping up to 10°C/20°F!). A long-sleeved shirt and long trousers should be worn or carried, for sun protection and for making your way through the prickly plants of the *maquis*. Depending on the season, you may also need an anorak, lightweight rainwear, woollies and gloves. Optional items include swimwear, a Swiss Army knife, plastic cups and flasks, insect repellent. Mineral water is sold almost everywhere in plastic half-litre bottles; *it is imperative that each walker carries at least a half-litre of water — a full litre in hot weather.*

Nuisances

We have never been bothered by dogs but, for peace of mind, you might like to invest in an ultrasonic **dog** deterrent: these 'Dog Dazers' are widely available on the web. Any **snakes** you may spot slithering out of your way will probably be harmless, but vipers (recognisable by the distinct triangular shape of the head) *do* exist (another good reason always to wear boots and long trousers). Take care if you move a log or stone, and *always* keep a look-out near drystone walls. Outside winter you may be plagued by an encyclopaedic array of **biting insects** — just when you are panting up a mountain or tucking into lunch. You may also encounter **beehives** along some of the routes; bees are not a problem if you keep your distance.

Waymarking, grading, safety

You will encounter **waymarking** on almost all the walks, but this is not necessarily helpful. Many routes have been waymarked over the years with different colours and symbols. Only the GR waymarking is meticulously maintained. Local councils change PR routes from year to year, often *without* removing the old waymarks.* Moreover, ***our walks do not always follow the waymarked routes***. At the top of each walk we mention current waymarking *at time of writing or updating*.

There are three principal types of route:

— **PR ('Petite Randonnée'):** local day walks, waymarked yellow
— **GR ('Grande Randonnée'):** long-distance walks, waymarked red/white (not to be confused with a red flash on a white paint background, which is local boundary marking, *not* route marking)
— **GRP ('Grande Randonnée du Pays'):** *recently developed* networks of circular/linear trails of varying lengths, designed to acquaint walkers with a particular region, waymarked red/yellow

Waymarking features common to all three routes:

— A *flash* (stripe of paint) indicates 'Route continues this way';
— A right- or left-angled flash (or an arrow) means 'Change direction';
— An 'X' means 'Wrong way'.

The walks have been **graded** for the deskbound person who nevertheless keeps reasonably fit. Our timings average 4km per hour on the flat, plus a generous 20 minutes for every 100m/300ft of ascent. None of the walks ascends more than about 600m/2000ft. *Do* check your timings against ours on a short walk before tackling one of the longer hikes. Remember that these are *neat walking times;* increase the overall time by *at least one-third* to allow for breaks, and *double it* in really hot weather.

Safety depends in great part on *knowing what to expect and being properly equipped*. For this reason we urge you to read through the *whole* walk description at your leisure *before* setting out, so that you have a mental picture of each stage of the route and the landmarks. On *most* of our walks you will encounter other people — an advantage if you get into difficulty. Nevertheless, we advise you **never** to walk alone.

Mercantour National Park

Several of our walks are set in the glorious Mercantour National Park (we alert you to this at the top of the relevant walks). Please, when walking or picnicking, be aware of the park rules:

■ No **motor vehicles** or **bicycles** are allowed, except on authorised roads and tracks;

---

*For this reason *never* follow local waymarks without the corresponding **up-to-date** IGN map or details from the tourist office (you may have to buy a book from them). You could find yourself on a dangerous path that has not been maintained for years. Beware, too: any walks described as '*sportif*' are always potentially hazardous!

- **Dogs** are not allowed — even on leads (this rule is unlikely to affect UK visitors, but has proved disappointing for those travelling in their own cars from the Continent);

- The picking (or digging up!) of **plants**, the collection of **minerals** or any other 'souvenirs' is strictly forbidden;

- **Hunting** is not allowed;

- Lighting **fires** is not allowed;

- **Camping** in tents or caravans is not allowed, but **'wild' camping** *is* permitted — at a distance of at least one hour on foot from the nearest road access;

- Playing **radios** is forbidden — as is making any other loud **noise**.

You can read more about the Mercantour at the national park's official website, www. mercantour.eu.

Signposting and waymarking in the Mercantour is carried out by the Conseil Général des Alpes-Maritimes and is just superb. See page 7 for their website details.

Maps

The **maps** in this book, adapted from IGN 1:25,000 maps, have been reproduced at a scale of 1:50,000 or larger. All the latest IGN maps (the 'Top 25' Series) show many local and long-distance walks. Older IGN maps ('Série Bleue') show *only* GR routes *or none at all:* it is very difficult to plan a short or circular walk using these maps, because they do not indicate permissive routes; 'on the ground' you may come up against barbed wire or a new housing estate. If Top 25 maps are not available, you will have to seek out up-to-date walks from the local tourist office (see Bibliography).

Below is a key to the symbols on our walking maps.

motorway	● ►	spring, tank, etc	🚐	bus stop
main road	∩	aqueduct	🚗	car parking
secondary road	⛪	church.chapel	🚂	railway station
minor or urban road	†	shrine or cross	🚋	tourist 'train'
motorable track	→	cemetery	▮□	castle, fort.ruins
other track	⊼	picnic tables	■	specified building
cart track, path, trail	⋏	pylon, transmitter	⚔∩	quarry, mine.cave
main walk 2→	—⌁—	electricity wires	⚑	windmill.stadium
alternative walk 2→	*i*	tourist office	• 312 ▮▶	walkers' signposts
watercourse, pipe	☀	mill	ⲓ	monument, tower
— 400 — height in metres	⛰	rock formation	△	campsite
	📷	best views	⛏	antiquity

Walk 1: ON THE ROOFTOPS OF NICE

Distance: about 8km/5mi; 3h
Grade: Quite easy, with little
ascent; descents (mostly on
steps) of about 300m/1000ft
overall. Yellow PR way-
marking. *IGN map 3742 OT*
Equipment: stout shoes will
suffice. *NB:* Take a plan of
Nice and information about
the Colline du Château (from
the tourist office). *No
refreshments available until
you return to the port*
Travel: town 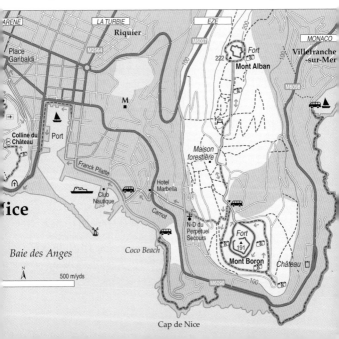 14 (www.
lignedazur.com) to the Mont
Boron bus terminus
Short walks
**1 Mont Boron and Mont
Alban.** 4km/2.5mi; 1h15min.

Easy. Follow the main walk to
the 1h15min-point, then take
 14 back to the centre.
2 Sentier Littoral. 4km/
2.5mi; 1h10min. Fairly easy,
but you must be agile and have
a head for heights (many ups/
downs, perhaps some scrambling over rocks). Town 30
to the 'Villa la Côte' stop past
the port. Almost opposite
descend steps to Coco Beach
and the coastal path (*Sentier
Littoral*). Follow it to Ville-
franche (halfway along, climb
steps to the M6098 and go
right until you can rejoin the
path down more steps). Take
town 80 back to Nice.

Dipping your toes into a Cote d'Azur walking
holiday couldn't be easier — you can start in the
city of Nice, by strolling round three mini-mountains
with beautiful woodlands and gardens, ancient remains
and breathtaking views.

Start the walk at the BUS
SHELTER on **Mont Boron**.
Walk to the AREA MAP at the
far side of the square. Two
paths are just to the right of
the map: take the tarred

footpath to the left, the **Sentier
du Cap de Nice**. This circles
Mont Boron below the old
fort, at first giving the fine
views shown overleaf. Olive
trees, holm oaks and pines

shade the path-side benches. Soon views open out over Cap Ferrat (Walk 4) and its lighthouse.

When you come to a road, the path continues just to the left of it (but first cross the road, to a lovely viewpoint over Ville-franche). Return to the path and follow it to a barrier. You are just 100m/yds short of your starting point, but it cannot be seen from here. Now take the trail that goes off left at a 90° angle, and walk round another barrier. This trail (**Circuit de Bellevue**) rounds the seaward side of the fort, circling the hill at a higher level.

When this second circuit is complete, go left on the road and follow it in a curve to the right, back to the square with the bus shelter (**35min**). Continue along the road past the AREA MAP, following signs for AUBERGE DE LA JEUNESSE. When the road curves right, take a tarred path off left (*ignore* the Allée du Bois Dormant just to the left of it). Rejoin the road and continue left uphill, quickly passing the MAISON FORESTIERE on the left. At a Y-fork go right for FORT DU MT ALBAN, then cut a bend off the road by walking left through a picnic area. In early spring this road is a blaze of yellow-flowering tree-spurge (*Euphorbia dendroides*). From the **Fort du Mont Alban** (**55min**) the views down over Villefranche and its bay are superb.

Return the same way to the AREA MAP in the square on Mont Boron (**1h15min**). Now descend the concreted steps on the right (the **Chemin des Crêtes**). Keep straight

From Mont Boron: the Colline du Château with its arched war memorial punctuates the coast between the port and the Promenade des Anglais.

Promenade des Anglais, quickly coming to the beautiful MEMORIAL to the dead of World Wars I and II on the right, its high arch carved into the **Colline du Château (2h)**. Keep rounding the hill, until you come to the lift (ASCENSEUR), and pay the small fee to ride up to the top. (If the lift happens to be out of action for repairs, you will have to climb the adjacent steps, 90m/300ft — or walk along the front a short way to catch the little white rubber-wheeled tourist train to the top.) Allow a good hour to potter about the top of the hill — not missing the Tour Bellanda (Naval Museum), the mosaics, the ruins of two cathedrals (10-12C and 14C) which once stood in the grounds of the Duke of Savoy's château, the beautiful waterfall fed by the Vésubie … and the views!

To return to town you *could* take the lift or adjacent steps or pick up the tourist train. We usually walk down via the cemeteries: take the steps below the waterfall, down to a road. Turn right, then take steps on the left signposted CIMETIERES, VIELLE VILLE. From the lowest (Roman Catholic) cemetery, take the road downhill to the right, then make a sharp hairpin bend to the left on Montée Eberlé. At the bottom, turn left for 100m, to **Place Garibaldi (3h)**. You can pick up a bus (or the tram) here — or, better still, have lunch in one of the restaurants facing this attractive square.

downhill through mixed woodlands, accompanied by wrens and robins, crossing straight over roads. In 10 minutes you pass to the right of the richly-decorated modern church (1927) of **Notre-Dame du Perpétuel Secours**. When you reach the Boulevard Carnot/M6098 *cross carefully (blind corners)*. The path continues just at the left side of the Hotel Marbella, heading towards the port and the Colline du Château. Make your way to the **Club Nautique** and continue opposite the COMMERCIAL PORT along the lovely residential Boulevard Franck Pilatte (🚌 20, 30, 32b). Follow the road inland (signposted 'Gare'), but turn left after about 40m/yds and walk to the PLEASURE PORT. Circle the port on the quays, then turn left towards the

Walk 2: MONT CHAUVE D'ASPREMONT

Distance: 10.5km/6.5mi; 3h25min

Grade: moderate ascent of 345m/1130ft and descent of 530m/1740ft. Good, but stony, paths and tracks underfoot. *Almost no shade.* Red and white GR, yellow PR waymarking. *IGN map 3742 OT*

Equipment: see page 72; refreshments available at Aspremont

Travel: 🚌 to Comte de Falicon, then town 🚌 76 from the adjacent Place de la Fontaine du Temple bus stop to Aspremont (St-Blaise bus); return on town 🚌 25 from Aire St-Michel to Le Rouret bus stop, then 🚌 from adjacent Henri Sappia tram stop (the most northerly stop on Tram Line 1) to Place Massena. All timetables/ plans from www.lignedazur.com

Alternative walk: Aspremont — Mont Chauve d'Aspremont — Aspremont. 9km/5.6mi; 2h55min. Grade

as main walk (ascent/descent of 345m/1130ft; access/return with 🚌 and 🚌 76 as above or by 🚗). Follow the main walk to the FORT (1h35min). Then walk back down the eight hairpin bends of the M214 (Route du Mont Chauve) and past the track you took on the way to the top. When you come to a barrier, take the wide waymarked path to the left. The waymarked route leads from here via the Baisse de Guigo back to Aspremont, and this is the route we have drawn on the map. But you could go a slightly different way at first: almost at once, you will come to a TUNNEL on the right. If you walk through it (no torch needed), you will exit looking straight across to the neighbouring (ruined) fort, Tourrette. Head right on a gravel track and turn left on another track after 200m/yds. At the Y-fork that follows almost immediately, bear left.

When you come to a yellow arrow pointing up to the right, *ignore it;* keep ahead on the lovely grassy path (you are back on the 'official' route), now making straight for Aspremont. Keep left again at the next Y-fork. Some 500m/yds further on, the path deteriorates and zigzags downhill over skiddy rubble. When you meet a cart track, turn left. On coming to a lane (**Chemin de la Bergerie**), follow it to the left. This takes you back to the GR51 path, which you follow back to Aspremont.

The flanks of Mont Chauve ('Bald Mountain') are virtually treeless, so all along this invigorating ridge walk you'll have unimpeded views. The sense of isolation is wonderful, too; it's hard to believe you're at the edge of the Riviera — until you take in the panorama from the massive fort!

Start out at the BUS STOP by the *hostellerie* in **Aspremont**. Walk back towards NICE on the M14 (the way the bus came in) for about 200m/yds. Past the CAR PARK, turn right down the **Chemin de la Vallière** (GR waymarks), taking concrete steps down into the **Magnan Valley**. Meet the M14 again in five minutes and go straight over, up a lane. In two minutes

keep ahead on a stony path. At a FORK ABOVE AN ISOLATED HOUSE (**10min**), turn sharp right uphill on the GR5. (The path straight ahead is the GR51, the return route for the Alternative walk.)

Rising on this stony path, you enjoy a fine view back over Aspremont on its conical hill and to the perched villages of Le Broc and Carros on the far side of the Var. Soon you pass a ruined building, **Fondalin** (**35min**) in a very pleasant, grassy setting. The path rises gently through golden grasses and *garrigues* until, when you are above Nice's crematorium on the main road, the sea comes into view ahead.

Les Faces (**50min**) is the next little ruin on route. Rising below abandoned hillside terracing, you come to a final ruin (**Les Templiers; 1h**) and reach a fork 200m/yds further on. Leave the GR here: turn sharp left uphill on a cart track, now following yellow waymarks and enjoying some fine views down over Nice and

View north to the snow-capped peaks of the Mercantour in winter

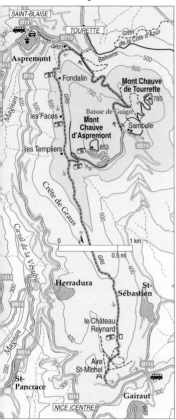

d'Aspremont (**1h35min**). The massive old FORT here, the last in a line of coastal defences stretching from Ste-Agnès (Walk 9) to Nice, is one of the best viewpoints in the area. While the coastal views are mesmerising, don't forget to look back north — up towards the Mercantour and the Alps! Take time, too, to walk down around the overgrown, grassy 'moat' between the inner and outer walls.

From the fort retrace your steps to the GR5 (**2h15min**). Now follow it to the left along the **Crête de Graus**. A slight rise takes you up to a COL in about 35 minutes. Ignore any minor or crossing paths; keep heading along the main path, towards a PYLON. You descend to the ruined walls of the **Château Reynard** (**3h**), a shady spot from where there is another fine view. The descent now becomes more pronounced for a short time, then levels out and comes to a T-junction. Go left, towards another PYLON. At the pylon, *ignore* the yellow PR route straight ahead; go right on the GR, which then turns left on a wide crossing path, into the olive groves and pines of a picnic area with tables (**Aire St-Michel**). On meeting a lane, follow it downhill past villas, to a ROUNDABOUT on **Avenue Jules Romains** (**3h25min**). The BUS SHELTER is on the far side of the roundabout, at the left of green iron gates. Don't be surprised if the bus goes into Falicon before heading south into Nice.

the coast. On approaching a rock face, follow the track in a U-bend to the left and then a sharp turn to the right (where a track goes straight ahead back towards Les Faces). The observatory on Mont Gros, as well as Mont Alban, Mont Boron and the port (Walk 1) are focal points on this stretch. The track contours above the rock face, with a fine view to the right along the Crête de Graus — the ridge you will follow back to Nice.

On meeting a road (**M214, Route du Mont Chauve**; **1h15min**), follow it uphill in tight hairpin bends to the SUMMIT of **Mont Chauve**

Walk 3: PEILLE AND PEILLON

Distance: 11.5km/7.1mi; 3h35min

Grade: moderate ascents/ descents of about 500m/1640ft overall. Little shade on the outgoing path; plenty on the return. Good yellow PR way-marking around Peillon; good sense of orientation needed for the many woodland paths from Peille, although they are waymarked. *IGN map 3742 OT*

Equipment: see page 72; walking stick. Refreshments available at Peille and Peillon

Travel: 🚂 to Peillon. Peille is served by 🚌 116 (www. departement06.fr/vous-deplacer-en-bus/lignes-et-horaires-3029.html), but current scheduling does not allow ample time for the circuit (see Alternative routes below).

Alternative routes: Peillon council has waymarked the **Circuit de Lourquière** and the **path from Peillon to La Grave**. If you are travelling by public transport you could take 🚌 116 (as above) to Peille, do the walk *in reverse* to Peillon (via the St-Pancrace Chapel and the Galambert Stream; well waymarked), then descend to La Grave for 🚌 360 (same website as bus 116) or 🚃 (www.ter-sncf.com: search under 'Peille').

O ld trails — some dating from Roman times — are followed in this circuit via the exquisite perched villages of Peille and Peillon. Which will you prefer? Peille thrills with its *via ferrata;* Peillon is picture-postcard perfect … and home to a top-class hotel, where you could enjoy a coffee on the terrace before the walk.

Start out at the 18th-century FOUNTAIN in **Peillon**. Walk up the paved steps behind it, then

turn left (⬛: PEILLE VILLAGE 2H). You pass an IRON CROSS and come into olive groves, with the **Lourquière** mountain rising on the right. At a first fork, keep ahead (⬛: PEILLE VILLAGE) and at the next go right (same ⬛). There is a beautiful view back to the thimble-like spur of Peillon now, and the path enters a gorge. When a METAL GATE blocks the path (**10min**), turn *sharp left* uphill.

Eventually the old stone-laid trail passes below the red-hued climbing rocks of the **Baus Roux**, then crosses the **Galambert Stream** on a FIRST STONE BRIDGE (**30min**). Four minutes later, ignore a path forking back to the right; keep ahead. Ignore another path off right and keep ahead over a SECOND STONE BRIDGE (**40min**; ⬛: CHAPELLE

81

ST-PANCRACE, PEILLE).
Continue uphill, straight towards the masts on the Cime de la Morgelle (but this 1076m-high peak rises well to the east of your ongoing route).

Tar comes underfoot in **Buampin (50min)**: keep uphill to a crossroads with a cul-de-sac sign ahead. Bend round to the right here on the Chemin de Buampin, past IRON GATES on the right. Meeting the D53 (**1h**), follow it 100m/yds to the right, then go sharp left on a path leaving from the left-hand side of a large PARKING AREA. This takes you up to a hairpin bend of the D22. Go left and after about 180m/yds take a footpath off right (there should be a CAIRN).

This pretty path passes the ruined **Chapelle St-Pancrace**, then descends gently through pines, back to the D53. Follow the road to the right. When the road bends right, by a rock promontory on the left (**1h25min**), your ongoing path dives down left just *before* the rock promontory. ***Note:***

this path is badly eroded, with unprotected drops to the left; you will get to Peille almost as quickly by continuing along the D53 — a safer option.

The path (or the road) gives you some superb views of Peille's pride and joy: its well-engineered *via ferrata* — climbing walls with iron hand-holds and suspension bridges over the dramatic **Farquin Gorge**. After crossing a stone bridge, the path rises to the MUSEUM at **Peille (1h45min)**. Once you have wandered around this beautifully-sited village strung out along the ravine walls, make your way to the round tower of the HOTEL DE VILLE and descend the adjacent steps (**Rue des Pous**). Keep zigzagging almost due south for about 10 minutes, until you reach the FINAL HAIRPIN BEND OF THE D53 below Peille, where your ongoing path descends concrete steps at the left (yellow waymarks; **2h**).

At a fork reached very quickly, take the descending path to the right (with a water pipe on your left). Keep downhill

Peillon, backed by the Lourquière mountain

The via ferrata *where it spans Peille's gorge*

across traces of hunters' paths, passing to the left of some houses in 10 minutes and crossing the **Farquin Stream** five minutes later (**2h15min**). *From here follow the notes carefully; it is easy to get lost in these beautiful, dense oak woods, as all the paths are waymarked in yellow!* Rise up from the stream, in five minutes ignoring a path back to the right. Pass to the left of a huge boulder which bears some yellow and red waymarks. Ten minutes up from the stream, ignore a large cairn on the right but, three minutes later, another TALL CAIRN marks an *important junction, where you must turn sharp left.* (The path straight ahead eventually joins a track, then descends to Paravielle and La Grave de Peille.) *Two minutes later, at a Y-fork, keep right.* In 10 minutes the path curls round to the right at the foot of a very large SCREE (**2h40min**). *If you have not reached this point within 30 minutes from crossing the Farquin stream, you have gone wrong.* Ten minutes later the

path runs through pines and tall grass higher up the ridge — a very attractive setting. You pass to the left of a BUILDING (**2h55min**), then curl left towards the crests. As you push through masses of broom *(this stretch can be very overgrown in spring)*, there are some open views down right to the huge quarry at La Grave.

Rise to a COL AND MARKER STONE 128 on the right (**3h05min**); keep straight ahead here, ignoring a path back to the right. Seven minutes later, at a Y-fork, keep right, quickly passing to the right of a CAIRN. From here the path descends gently, eventually coming to a fork: keep straight ahead (☞: PEILLON VILLAGE). A stone-laid trail takes you to the next fork, where you go right (same ☞). At a third fork, keep straight on, retracing your steps past the IRON CROSS to the FOUNTAIN in Peillon (**3h35min**). Before leaving, be sure to visit the **Chapelle des Pénitents Blancs** with its Renaissance frescoes.

Walk 4: AROUND CAP FERRAT

Distance: 8km/5mi; 2h45min
Grade: easy, with ups and downs of about 130m/425ft, *but potentially dangerous when wet or very windy*. Limited shade. *No waymarks, but easily followed. IGN map 3742 OT*
Note: When you meet the M125 near the end of the walk, you can first turn *left*, to visit the Ephrussi de Rothschild Foundation, with its beautiful gardens and Ile de France Museum (paid entrance).
Equipment: see page 72; swimming things. Refreshments available at St-Jean-Cap-Ferrat
Travel: 🚗 or town 🚌 81 (www.lignedazur.com) to St-Jean-Cap-Ferrat

Short walk: Pointe de St-Hospice. 2.8km/1.7mi; 1h10min; easy). Follow the main walk to the 1h-point, then return to the port.
Alternative walk: Beaulieu — Cap Ferrat — Beaulieu. 13km/8mi; 3h55min. Grade as main walk. Access: 🚗, 🚌 100 (www.departement06.fr/vous-deplacer-en-bus/lignes-et-horaires-3029.html) or 🚆 (www.ter-sncf.com) to Beaulieu. From the casino follow the seafront walkway (**Promenade Maurice Rouvier**) south along the coast to St-Jean-Cap-Ferrat; the Villa Kerylos is en route. After the main walk, return the same way to Beaulieu.

L ovely any time of year, this walk is especially enjoyable on a bright and bracing winter's day. You'll walk below the exotic gardens of some of the most exquisite properties on the Riviera, with far-reaching views out to sea and for miles east and west along the 'Azure Coast'.

Begin the walk overlooking the PORT at **St-Jean-Cap-Ferrat**. Walk south, then east, round the port, then go up AVENUE JEAN MERMOZ, keeping the Hotel Voile d'Or on your left. Take steps on the left down to the **Paloma Beach** restaurant. Here you pick up a coastal walkway running round the **Pointe de St-Hospice**, with fine views over to Eze, La Turbie, the Tête de Chien, Monaco and Cap Martin.

Approaching the port at St-Jean-Cap-Ferrat on the seafront promenade from Beaulieu, with the Pointe de St-Hospice in the background

After rounding the point, take steps on the right (⊓) up to the 19th-century **Chapelle St-Hospice** with its huge bronze-painted statue of Virgin and Child. An 18th-century TOWER is adjacent, but is on private land and not fully visible.

Then return to the coastal path and turn right. Beyond the **Pointe du Colombier**, the path enters a lovely pine wood (**La Pinède**) at the edge of a little bay (**Les Fossettes**), then meets a road at a T-junction (**1h**). Turn left here. *(But for the Short walk, turn right immediately after turning left, and retrace your outgoing route back to the port.)* Follow the road past the next little bay, **Les Fosses**.

At the next T-junction, eight minutes later, go left and walk round a metal barrier. You pick up the coastal walkway again and begin to round **Cap Ferrat**. Trailing superb views inland (and dodging the sea-spray), now you can really stride out, while watching the

yachts and high-speed ferries sailing to and from the nearby ports of Villefranche and Nice. The path passes above many pretty little inlets, and below the LIGHTHOUSE (**1h40min**; paid entrance when open to the public, if you decide to climb up to it).

After skirting the Lido apartments by road, the path ends at the **Plage de Passable** (**2h30min**). Climb the steps at the left of the beach restaurant, cross straight over a road and go up more steps. At the next road, walk left for 160m/yds, then go right, up an alley. You emerge on the main M125 (**Avenue Denis Séméria**); the TOURIST OFFICE is on your left. Walk to the BUS SHELTER opposite (to the right) and take another alley just to the right of it. Rejoining Avenue Séméria lower down, follow it against the one-way traffic back to the PORT at **St-Jean**. A BUS STOP is opposite the MAIRIE (**2h45min**), and there are cafés and restaurants galore, some of them open year-round.

Walk 5: RAVIN DU MAL INFERNET

NB: Some paths in the Esterel may be closed between 21 June and 30 September if fire risk is high. See www.paca.gouv.fr/files.massif (map updated daily).
See map pages 88-89
Distance: 7.5km/4.7mi; 1h55min
Grade: easy, with an ascent of under 100m/330ft near the end of the walk. However, the tracks and paths are stony underfoot, and there is almost no shade. Red/white GR way-marking. *IGN map 3544 ET*
Equipment: see page 72; swimming things. No refreshments available beyond Agay
Travel: 🚌 to the parking area at the Col de Belle-Barbe,

north of Agay (Car tour 1). No 🚌 access.
Alternative walk: Sommet des Grosses Grues and Balcons de la Côte d'Azur. 18km/11.2mi; about 7h; moderate-strenuous, with ascents/descents of about 550m/1800ft overall. Access as main walk. Follow the main walk to the Lac de l'Ecureuil (55min), then continue on the GR51 to the Col Notre-Dame and the Sommet des Grosses Grues. Return the same way — or, from the Col Notre-Dame, vary the return (see lilac lines on the map). Tremendous coastal views throughout; carry *plenty of food and water.*

The crystalline Esterel is as old as the Maures (see page 58). You don't have to be a geologist to marvel at the colours of these porphyry rocks, with a wealth of minerals sparkling in rainbow hues. The ideal time to visit is early spring: the hillsides are aglow with flowers, and the stream, just a trickle in summer, is full.

Start out at the **Col de Belle-Barbe**: from a WHITE PILLAR, head across the road (☞: LAC DE L'ECUREUIL). Follow the earthen track; the dramatic outline of the Pic de l'Ours is straight ahead. Beyond a small lake, the boulder-strewn **Ravin du Grenouillet** opens up on your right. When you come to an old parking area, continue downhill to the left on the stony track, to cross the bed of the **Mal Infernet Stream** on a concrete FORD (**15min**). Just past here, ignore a wide path off right (to the Rocher du Gravier). As you round a bend, the **Ravin du Mal Infernet** reveals its tortured landscape: jagged red rocks rise on both sides of the limpid stream. Just after passing a SPRING on the right (**30min**), you reach one of the prettiest settings on

the walk (*in spring*): the stream is dammed to form a glassy pool, which spills over into a lovely waterfall. Soon the banks slope gently down to the stream — an ideal spot to swim or picnic. Two-three minutes later the GR51 climbs up left to the Col Aubert; this will be our return route. Keep ahead; in another five minutes the gorge curls round and you look straight ahead to the Mamelon de l'Ecureuil, a high rounded hill. A few holm and cork oaks provide welcome shade. At a fork, turn left downhill and cross a BRIDGE (**50min**). The Pic de l'Ours, with its fractured crown, rises on the right here, as you continue into a dramatic 'wild-west' setting. Soon the sound of rushing water heralds your approach to the tiny **Lac de l'Ecureuil**

*The Ravin du Mal Infernet (top),
view across the Ravin des Lentisques
to Cap Roux and St-Pilon (middle),
the Mal Infernet stream (bottom)*

(Squirrel Lake; **55min**),
another lovely picnic spot.
Several other waymarked trails
continue north and east from
here; see the Alternative walk
or IGN map 3544 ET.
Return from the lake *and watch
carefully in the undergrowth* for
where the GR leaves the track
(**1h10min**). Cross the river on
a metal mesh bridge and follow
the stony footpath up the far
side, climbing quickly, with
beautiful views down over the
stream. Accompanied by
butterflies galore, climb to the
Col Aubert (**1h25min**),
where the GR goes right up to
the Col du Baladou. Leave the
GR at this crossroads of paths:
go left along a flat stretch of
shadeless path. Watch out now
for the stunted strawberry trees
(*Arbutus unedo*) with their
unmistakeable red fruits (edible
but sour). Ignore the path off
to the right just below the **Pic
du Baladou**; continue to the
left. From the highest point in
this climb there is a fine view
across the Ravin des Len-
tisques to the twin summits of
Cap Roux, rising above a bib
of trees. The Pic du Cap Roux
(453m) is on the left; Le
St-Pilon (445m; not within
our map area) on the right.
Now the wide stony path
descends, with a good view
over your outgoing track and
the stream bed down on the
left. The green basins and red
rock folds of the Esterel rise all
around you; pale olive-green
porphyry rock is underfoot.
The Pic du Baladou path
comes in from the right, and in
a trice you are back at the **Col
de Belle-Barbe** (**1h55min**).

Walk 6: CIRCUIT ABOVE THEOULE-SUR-MER

NB: Some paths in the Esterel may be closed between 21 June and 30 September if fire risk is high. See www.paca.gouv.fr/ files.massif (map updated daily).
Distance: 8km/5mi; 2h20min from Théoule centre; 12km/ 7.4mi; 3h40min from Théoule's railway station
Grade: easy, with an ascent/ descent of 130m/425ft overall. Some of the tracks and paths are stony underfoot; *little*

shade. Red and white GR, yellow PR waymarking. *IGN map 3544 ET*
Equipment: see page 72; swimming things. Refreshments available at Théoule
Travel: 🚗 (Car tour 1), 🚆 (www.ter-sncf. com) or 🚌 620 (www.departement06.fr/ vous-deplacer-en-bus/lignes-et-horaires-3029. html) to Théoule-sur-Mer (but see 'Distance' above).

One of the advantages of a break — even a weekend — on the Côte d'Azur is the excellent public transport. There's a good week's walking in this book for which you won't need a hire car — especially if you're based between Cannes and Nice. This little gem is a perfect example but, by referring to the paths on the map highlighted in lilac (all waymarked), you can make up any combination of routes. We like to do this walk by train, but you can also return by bus from the beachside restaurant at the end of the walk.

Our walk begins at Théoule's RAILWAY STATION, 1km north of the village on the D6098. While you *could* just take this main road south to Théoule centre, we like to follow the GR51: turn right out of the station and follow the main road south for 150m/yds. Take the first right uphill, crossing the railway, then the first left downhill (🠔). Follow this lane in a little valley, round a hairpin bend to the left and back to the D6098. Turn right into **Théoule-sur-Mer (40min)**. Then turn right off the D6098 at signs for *MAIRIE/POSTE*. Pass both (on your left) and keep ahead. When this street makes a hairpin turn to the left (back to the D6098), continue ahead on a track behind a barrier (🠔: *COL DE THEOULE*), rising above the railway line, into the Esterel.
Watch carefully for where the

GR footpath heads right, off the track (**1h10min**; you can see the railway entering the **Tunnel des Saumes** not far ahead); follow the GR, initially alongside the railway, and then

In February mimosas brighten the balcony path above the coast.

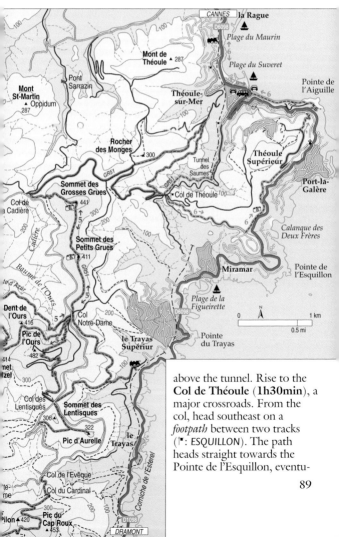

above the tunnel. Rise to the **Col de Théoule (1h30min)**, a major crossroads. From the col, head southeast on a *footpath* between two tracks (▐: *ESQUILLON*). The path heads straight towards the Pointe de l'Esquillon, eventually widening into a road (Avenue Matisse). When you come to a junction some 40m/130ft above the D6098 (**2h**), turn left on a 'balcony' footpath and walk northeast, with fine coastal views, eventually to **Port-la-Galère**. Tarmac comes underfoot again. Just before a junction, turn sharp left uphill on a track (Boulevard des Alpes; **⌐**: *POINTE DE L'AIGUILLE, THEOULE*). Follow this until it curves west, by a wooden barrier on the right. Turn sharp right downhill past the barrier and, from a small open space with an area map, take the zigzag path down towards the coast. Turn left on the tarmac road at the bottom and keep forking downhill to the D6098. Turn right and walk some 100m/yds to the brow of the hill, then take steps on the left down to the superb rock formations at the **Pointe de l'Aiguille** (**2h45min**). From here follow coastal paths to **Théoule-sur-Mer** (**3h**). You emerge by a beachside *RESTAURANT* with a *BUS SHELTER*, from where you can retrace your outgoing route back to the *STATION* (**3h40min**).

Walk 7: View east from the Cap du Dramont, to the Pointe de Baumette and the Pic du Cap Roux

Walk 7: CAP DU DRAMONT

See photograph opposite
Distance: 5.5km/3.4mi; 2h
Grade: fairly easy ascents/
descents of about 200m/650ft
overall, but you must be sure-
footed. Some signs; yellow PR
waymarking. *IGN map 3544 ET*
Equipment: see page 72;

swimming things. Refresh-
ments available at Port du
Poussaï and Camp Long
Travel: 🚌, 🚐 8 (www.agglo
bus-cavem.com/horaires —
choose 'Ligne 8') or 🚆
(www.ter-sncf.com) to Cap du
Dramont

W ith the exception of Le Trayas, Dramont's red
porphyry rock *calanques* are the most beautiful
on the coast. When the sun sparkles on the azure sea
through the shimmering pines, this landscape is
unbelieveably stunning.

Start out at the LE DRAMONT
RAILWAY STATION: cross the
D1098 to the monument
commemorating the landing of
the US Army's 36th Division
on 15 August 1944 (car
parking), then walk east
towards Agay. At the roundabout, turn right on the
Boulevard du Sémaphore.
After some 300m/yds, turn left
just in front of house No 245,
quickly coming to a BARRIER,
beyond which are some
walkers' ⛳.
Heading right towards
POUSSAI, the square tower on
the **Ile d'Or** quickly becomes a
focal point. Go down to the
little **Port du Poussaï**, where a
⛳: CIRCUIT DU CAP, signals the
official start of the walk (yellow
waymarks). Take a break on
the red rocks at the **Pointe du
Dramont**, before rising above
the largest of the coves, the
Mare Règue. Turn left up a
path here, to a PASS between
the two highest 'peaks' on the
cape.
First turn left to visit the
Sémaphore (with viewpoint;
50min); then return to the
pass and walk up to the
Belvédère de la Batterie. Both
are superb viewpoints down
over the deeply-etched coves,
southwest to the Golfe de

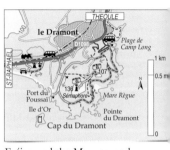

Fréjus and the Maures, and
northeast to the Esterel and the
Golfe de la Napoule.
Return to the circuit path and
continue to the **Plage de
Camp Long** (**1h35min**; BUS
STOP), where you can take a
break at the beachside
RESTAURANT.
The main walk returns from
here to the BARRIER (⛳) on the
south side of the beach, from
where you continue the circuit
on the northern side of the
cape, back to the BARRIER at the
start of the circuit. From there
retrace your steps to the
RAILWAY STATION (**2h**).
But if you came by train, you
could instead follow the
concreted coastal path from
Camp Long to Agay (also **2h**)
and catch the train there. (This
path runs — with some
interruptions — all the way to
Antibes; we take in part of it at
Théoule, on Walk 6.)

91

Walk 8: FROM LA TURBIE TO EZE-BORD-DE-MER

NB: La Trophée des Alpes is closed on Mondays.
Distance: 8km/5mi; 3h15min
Grade: easy ascent of 155m/510ft, but strenuous descent of 600m/1970ft. Little shade. Yellow PR waymarking. *IGN map 3742 OT*
Equipment: see page 72; walking stick(s). Refreshments available at La Turbie and Eze
Travel: 🚌 116 (www.departe ment06.fr/vous-deplacer-en-bus/lignes-et-horaires-3029. html) to La Turbie; return by 🚌 100 (same website) or 🚆 (www.ter-sncf.com) from Eze-Bord-de-Mer
Shorter walk: La Turbie — Eze-Village. 6km/3.7mi; 2h20min. Fairly easy, but a steep descent of 280m/920ft. Follow the main walk to Eze-Village and return by 🚌 112

(same website as 🚌 116 above). This avoids the final 320m/1050ft of descent. Perhaps visit the exquisite Jardin Exotique at Eze.
Alternative walk: La Turbie — Maison de la Nature — La Turbie. 8km/5mi; 2h50min. Easy ascent/descent of 155m/510ft. 🚗 (Car tour 2) or 🚌 116 (as above) to La Turbie. Follow the main walk to the 1h40min-point, then continue along the corniche track, eventually forking left to a water tank on the **Cime de la Forna**. Fork left again, to descend a stony path back to the reservoirs, and retrace your steps to La Turbie. (Optional detour: take in part of the **Sentier botanique**, with a *table d'orientation*).

O n this walk you will enjoy some of the finest views on the whole of the Riviera. The main walk rises gently along the north side of the Grande Corniche crest, with superb views up to the mountains, before crossing the shoulder — to a magnificent coastal panorama. From here the main walk dives south, with plunging views over Eze and Cap Ferrat, while the Alternative walk contours east along the old corniche military track, with coastal views towards Italy.

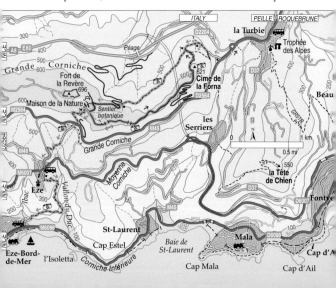

Eze-Village

The walk begins at the MAIRIE on the main road (D2564, the **Grande Corniche**) in **La Turbie**. Cross over the road to the Hotel Napoléon, then turn left. After 450m/yds, at the ROUNDABOUT, ignore the D2204 off right to the motorway; go straight across towards 'Nice' and walk past a cylindrical PILLAR WITH AN IRON CROSS on the top (on your right). Some 250m/yds from the roundabout, turn right up the **Chemin de la Forna** (10min; ⊮). There are fine views back to the Trophée des Alpes as you climb. As the tarmac runs out, keep straight ahead on a cart track (⊮: CIME DE LA FORNA), to pass to the right of a RESERVOIR (20min). Just before a second, square reservoir, turn left up another stony cart track (⊮). In two minutes keep straight ahead (⊮: FORT DE LA REVERE). *(The Alternative walk returns via the 'Cime de la Forna' path to the left here.)*

Now a lovely path through tall grass takes you along the northern flanks of the **Grande Corniche**, just below the crest. You look north to Utelle,

where the chapel shown on page 25 teeters on the edge of the cliff, and the mountains of the Mercantour. The Fort de la Revère crowns the rise to the west, above two forestry park buildings. From here the frenetic jockeying for position at the motorway toll booths below seems a world away. On meeting the U-bend of a track, turn left uphill (⊮: FORT DE LA REVERE). You emerge at a large *doline* (sinkhole) and the **Maison de la Nature** (1h25min), with an interesting little museum, well-landscaped gardens, and picnic tables. Before continuing towards Eze, walk downhill to the coastal overlook (with benches) and follow the corniche track for short way. After five minutes, just before the FIRST TUNNEL, a **Sentier botanique** (with a *table d'orientation*) turns sharply up to the left — a possible detour. Continue through a SECOND TUNNEL (1h40min), to take in the superb coastal panorama. *(The Alternative walk continues along this track.)*

From the second tunnel retrace your steps to the Maison de la

93

further junctions, until you meet the **Grande Corniche** again (**2h05min**). Cross *carefully*, turn right for 20m/yds, then turn left down a lane, the **Chemin Serre de Forque** (◄). The shade of pines is welcome here, but the descent is *very* steep. Keep straight down, whether by tar, path or steps, until you meet the M6007, the **Moyenne Corniche**, opposite the entrance to **Eze-Village** (**2h20min**; BUS SHELTER, CAFÉS). Take a break here before, knees a-tremble, you begin the final descent.

Cross the road and head up into Eze, passing the TOURIST OFFICE on your right. Just past the FRAGONARD PERFUMERY SHOP on your left, you will turn left down the **Chemin Frédéric Nietzche** (◄: EZE MER). But first join the crowds and walk on through this enchanting village — to visit the tropical gardens, church, and White Penitent's Chapel. Just above the chapel is the Nid d'Aigle, a super restaurant for a meal or snack.

Nietzche's wide old trail (he apparently climbed it every morning from his house on the coast) descends in gentle zigzags through a surprisingly wild valley (**Vallon du Duc**) above deeply-cut *calanques*. Eventually the path turns right, crosses a COL (**2h50min**) and makes the final descent — with fine views over Cap Ferrat. When you meet the M6098 (**Corniche Inférieure**) at **Eze-Bord-de-Mer**, turn right to the BUS STOP. The RAILWAY STATION and another TOURIST OFFICE are just a short way further along, on the south side of the road (**3h15min**).

Nature and start walking up the road towards the **Fort de la Revère**. But after less than 100m/yds, turn left down a footpath (◄: EZE-VILLAGE). This pretty path descends through tall grass above some luxurious villas. On coming to a concrete drive, follow it downhill to the right. Keep right, downhill, at

Walk 9: FROM STE-AGNÈS TO CASTELLAR

Distance: 7km/4.3mi; 2h35min
Grade: easy-moderate ups and downs — about 500m/1640ft of descent overall and 270m/885ft of ascent (of which 200m is at the end of the walk). Red and white GR waymarking. *IGN map 3742 OT*
Equipment: see page 72; refreshments available at Ste-Agnès, Monti and Castellar
Travel: 🚌 10 from Menton bus station to Ste-Agnès; return by 🚌 6 from Castellar to Menton; for both buses see www.zestbus.fr/Pratique/Lignes-et-horaires
Short walk: Ste-Agnès — Monti. 4.5km/2.8mi; 1h35min. Easy. Follow the walk to Monti and return by 🚌 15 (www.zestbus.fr/Pratique/Lignes-et-horaires) — this avoids the final ascent into Castellar.

The tangle of old cobbled lanes at Ste-Agnès, woven below arched passageways, is strongly evocative of medieval times. But although this 'highest of Europe's coastal villages' has always been strategically important (the fort was the most southerly defence of the Maginot Line), it wasn't accessible by road until 1933. This walk mostly follows the undulations of an old mule trail to Castellar — another perched village and, like St-Agnès, home to many artists and artisans.

The walk begins at the **Col St-Sébastien**, 200m/yds below **Ste-Agnès**, at the junction with the D22 to the Col de Gorbio. There's a medieval CHAPEL here, a FOUNTAIN, and a barrage of signposts. Follow the old cobbled footpath descending below the chapel, the GR51 (➤: *LA VIRETTE, MONTI, CASTELLAR*). Sometimes horses are kept in this area; if you encounter any electrified fences, use the insulated handles to open and close the gates. As you descend into the wilderness of the **Borrigo Valley**, it's hard to believe that you're just a short way inland from the busy coast. You pass a stand of cypresses that once gave welcome shade to travellers ascending to Ste-Agnès and descend to the grassy banks of the stream, a lovely place to while away an hour … or three! *(Be sure to turn sharp right here; do not follow what may look like a more obvious path straight on.)* When you come to the stream crossing, you may find horses slaking their thirst and encounter another electrified fence. Look ahead now to your destination — the honey-hued buildings of Castellar, strung along a ridge.

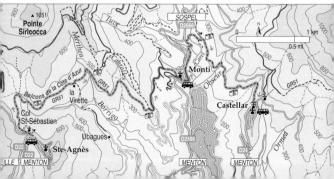

The walk follows centuries-old cobbled mule trails.

You pass through a rock chaos in a grove of trees (obviously a popular shady picnic spot) and then another rock chaos. Beyond a small stream bed, you rise to the ruined hamlet of **La Virette** (35min). Descending steeply from the ruins, watch carefully for the GR 'change of direction' sign and turn *sharp left* downhill, *ignoring* any yellow waymarks. Cross another stream (in the **Ravin de Merthea**) and rise quite steeply, past a short narrow section with a drop to the right. As you head southeast on the far side of this ravine, look back to Ste-Agnès, where its strategic position on the rocky escarpment is evident. Your eye will also be drawn to the motorway below, and the Monastère de l'Annonciade at Menton. Dip into yet another little gulley, the **Ravin de Cabrolles** — a cool glen in summer, where ivy twines round the trees. Having climbed up the far side, a wide cobbled trail comes in from the left behind you; here you look straight down on Cap Martin (Walk 10). Straight away you come you come onto a bulldozed track: *follow the GR waymarks*

carefully on the next stretch, as there are several bulldozed tracks in this area. Basically, you should be contouring, descending slightly, until a fork to the right takes you back onto a path.

On coming to a concrete-surfaced T-junction, turn right. Steps take you down to the CHURCH at **Monti** (1h35min). Cross over to the AUBERGE PIERROT PIERRETTE (closed at time of checking), then turn sharp left just past the BUS SHELTER; your concrete path continues just behind it (although it looks as if you are walking straight into private property!). Descend towards an industrial area but, just before reaching it, be sure to go straight ahead along a track (just past a huge pylon). Walk to the left of a glass and breeze-block wall (a private swimming pool).

Now you start to round the final large valley before Castellar, the **Torrent Careï**. Immediately after crossing a stream, keep left uphill at a Y-fork. Then, just as you start to rise on concrete steps, fork right on a path, through a pretty, wooded section. Cross another stream and, on meeting a concrete road, follow it uphill to the left. But a short way up, fork sharp right (⌐: CASTELLAR). This takes you down a concrete path. Cross the main stream and, at a fork, keep left uphill (⌐: CASTELLAR 1H). But fork right just 15 paces along. As you rise you can look north to the Caramel Viaduct on the far side of the road to Sospel (see Car tour 2 and page 168). The path climbs in easy zigzags, sometimes through vineyards, and with an excellent view to Castellar on the approach.

On coming to a crossing concrete lane, turn left uphill to a CHAPEL on the **Avenue** **St-Anton** in **Castellar** (**2h35min**). Follow the road uphill to the right, then take steps up right, into the heart of the village. At the top of the steps there is an IRON CROSS; opposite is the BUS STOP.

Castellar, like Sospel, is aglow with the warm, rich colours of nearby Italy.

Walk 10: CAP MARTIN

Distance: 5km/3.1mi; 1h45min

Grade: easy, with gentle ups and downs, mostly on a concrete walkway. *IGN map 3742 OT*

Equipment: see page 72; bathing things. Refreshments at the railway station café; cafés and restaurants along the coast from Cap Martin to Menton

Travel: 🚃 or 🚂 (www.ter-sncf.com) to the Roquebrune-Cap-Martin railway station. Or 🚌 100 (www.departe ment06.fr/vous-deplacer-en-bus/lignes-et-horaires-3029.html) to the '2ème Escalier' (a bus stop on the D6007 by steps descending 80m/260ft to the railway station, so allow extra time for the descent/ascent.

Note: You could begin by visiting the hill village of Roquebrune, with the oldest feudal castle in France, and then take steps (the 'Escalier Saft') 250m/820ft down to the coast, to begin the walk (🚌 21 from Menton bus station to Roquebrune old town, alight at the stop called 'Lavoir'; www.zestbus.fr/Pratique/Lignes-et-horaires)

Cap-Martin is to Menton what Cap Ferrat is to Nice — both exclusive enclaves of the seriously wealthy. But their coastal paths are accessible to everyone, so for a while you can be 'master of all you survey' — the princely views are free.

Start the walk at the *RAILWAY STATION* for **Roquebrune-Cap-Martin**. Cross the bridge over the railway, then turn left and make your way over to the coastal path, **Le Corbusier** (**5min**). Trailing fine views

back to Monaco, you pass several spurs down to jumping-off points where you could swim but, remember, the sea is at least 10m/30ft deep here. (The path is named in memory of the architect, who *drowned* while swimming off these rocks.)

You pass below the **Villa Cyrnos**, once the home of the Empress Eugénie, where Winston Churchill came to dine and paint. Finally you skirt the grounds of the exclusive Résidence du Cap hotel, then round the tip of the cape, with fine views over to Menton.

The path ends at the **Boulevard Winston Churchill** (**55min**). Retrace your steps from here. With views focussing on Monaco, Cap Ferrat, the Tête de Chien, La Turbie and the perched village of Roquebrune, return to the *RAILWAY STATION* for **Roquebrune-Cap-Martin** (**1h45min**).

Obviously another option is to walk on into Menton, from where there are frequent buses and trains east and west.

View north from the coastal path to Menton and the peaks east of Sospel

Walk 11: ABOVE SOSPEL

See also photograph pages 16-17

Distance: 9km/5.6mi; 3h

Grade: moderate, with ascents/descents of 430m/1410ft overall. Red and white GR, yellow PR waymarking. *IGN map 3741 ET*

Equipment: see page 72; refreshments available at Sospel

Travel: 🚗 (Car tour 2) or 🚌 15 from Menton (www.zestbus.fr/Pratique/Lignes-et-horaires) or 🚃 (www.ter-sncf.com) to Sospel

Short walk: Puella circuit. 6km/3.7mi; 1h35min. Easy, with a gradual ascent and short, fairly steep descent of 90m/295ft. While you *could* walk the 'official' Puella circuit up to Mont Agaisen (see lilac highlighting on the map), our version is just a very easy ramble overlooking the eastern Bévéra basin, with fine views back to Sospel. Follow the main walk to the school, then turn right (☞: *LA PUELLA*). Keep along the lane marked with yellow flashes, ignoring all turn-offs, until you come to ☞98, then turn down right for *SOSPEL PAR D2204*. This VTT route is very eroded, but quickly takes you to the D2204. Turn left and, at a junction, go right on the D93 in the **Nièya Valley** towards *VENTIMIGLIA*, passing **Le Palais du Golf**, a large hotel which has been in sight throughout the walk. After 600m/yds, at ☞102, turn right on the GR510. A shady path and then a cart track take you to the lovely farm of **St-Gervais**. When the way forks just before the farm, take the upper track through the buildings (there may be vicious dogs on the lower track). Continue back to the D2204 and the centre of **Sospel**.

T wo things always delight us at Sospel — the wonderful freshness in the air and the Italianate atmosphere of the town, especially around the Place de la Cathédrale and along the banks of the rushing Bévéra River, where the richly-painted buildings are decorated with *trompe l'œil* façades. Mont Agaisen affords you a fine view over the whole setting.

Start out in the centre of **Sospel** by crossing the *road* bridge over the **Bévéra River**. You look over to the right, to the 11th-century footbridge with its rebuilt toll tower (now the tourist office), flag a-flutter. Turn half-right on the far side (☞70), and follow this road for 200m/yds, then take steps up left to the Art Deco SCHOOL (☞72: *COL DE L'AGAISEN*), from where you follow the red/white-waymarked GR52. Turn off the road where it makes a hairpin bends to the right: go straight ahead on a lane (☞74; **15min**), following the GR towards *BAISSE DE FIGUEIRA*. Ignore two drives into houses almost immediately; keep left on a wide cart track. At the three-way fork that follows, take the middle route. There are lovely views left over olive groves and hillside terracing. At a Y-fork 10 minutes later, keep right. Soon the path moves into welcome shade and gently

Fountain in Place St-Nicholas, on the north side of the footbridge in Sospel

climbs a dry stream bed via a series of zigzags. As you rise, there's a spectacular view south across the Sospel basin. Eventually a very short steep final burst brings you up to a three-way junction (**1h**). Take the road straight ahead uphill here. Some 250m/yds further up, at ⌐75, turn sharp right uphill for *BAISSE DE FIGUEIRA*. A second ⌐75 follows almost immediately: turn right for *COL DE L'AGAISEN*, where the GR52 to Baisse de Figueira curls up sharply to the left. From here the path undulates (keep straight ahead over a crossing path nine minutes along), finally descending to ⌐84. Turn right here towards *COL DE L'AGAISEN*. This beautiful

section of path contours below pines and oaks.

On reaching a maze of paths and tracks at the **Col de l'Agaisen** (⌐83; **1h30min**), you'll find a steep path straight ahead. We suggest you ignore it: it's often used by VTTs. Instead cut across to a Y-junction of lanes (where you'll find another ⌐83) and head left, up to the *BLOCK-HOUSE* at the summit of **Mont Agaisen** (751m/2465ft; **1h50min**). Alpine hunters and riflemen were stationed here for many years from the late 1800s until 1939, to protect the border. There's a fine view of the Sospel basin … and you *might* see some colourful hang-gliders.

101

The forest paths and cobbled trails are mostly good underfoot, and in autumn Venetian sumac lights up the woodlands.

contours along the north side of the summit, then heads southeast through a sweetly-scented pine forest. The soft pine needles underfoot make this section very pleasant (photograph bottom left). You have a beautiful view down over the Short walk route in the Nièya Valley and out to the Bévéra Valley running through comfortable mountain folds towards Olivetta in Italy. The narrow but good path is also used by VTTs and so is skiddy in places. After the path curves southwest you pass a barn punctuated with cypress trees, then follow the path straight over a road. When you meet the road again, follow it to the right and, after under 200m/yds, go left downhill. The path passes a little chapel with stained-glass windows.

The final descent is along the lovely stone-laid mule trail shown above (right). A concrete ramp drops you down to ⌐83 (2h50min); behind and to the left is the lane followed in the 'Puella' circuit (Short walk). From here you have a beautiful view to the church with its *trompe l'œil* façade, together with two smaller churches. Back at the SCHOOL, turn left down the concrete steps, to the centre of **Sospel (3h)**.

From here retrace your steps to ⌐83 and now turn right on the path just below the lane. When you come to yet another ⌐83 at a Y-fork, go half-right for SOSPEL VIA GR52A. This path

102

Walk 12: CIME DE L'ARPIHA

Distance: 9km/5.6mi; 2h40min
Grade: easy-moderate, with ascents/descents of about 280m/920ft; good tracks and paths. The scramble to the Arpiha summit demands some agility. Yellow PR way-marking. *IGN map 3741 ET*
Equipment: see page 72; refreshments available at Turini

Travel: 🚗 (Car tour 2) or 🚌 340/360 from Nice to the Col de Turini (Mon/Wed/Thu *on demand:* tel 0800 060106 — it helps to speak French — no later than 4pm the day before you want to travel to arrange; see www.departement06.fr/documents/Import/servir-les-habitants/paillons.pdf).

Turini! One of the first places we make for when we arrive at Nice. Surrounded by magnificent forests of firs and spruce, this eyrie is as silent and refreshing as a Christmas morning snowfall ... except when there's a motor rally on the famous hairpin road! Nearby are the gold-green mountains of the Authion (see panel page 23), the backdrop for this walk.

Start out at the **Col de Turini**: walk north on the D68 (Authion road, signposted CAMP D'ARGENT). After 700m/yds, at ⌐234 (**15min**), turn left. Follow this motorable track to the **Vacherie de Mantégas** (⌐235). From July to September you can sample and buy local cheeses here. From the dairy farm continue towards L'ARPIHA on wide track (⌐: ITINERAIRE). When you come to a CLEARING at spot height 1648 (**30min**), signs point straight ahead to L'Arpiha. But we take the fork *half-left* here. This shady and mostly grassy path undulates along the south side of the Scoubayoun ridge. Breaks in

the trees afford glimpses down left over Turini and the hairpin road. Be sure to keep right uphill at a fork 15 minutes along (as waymarked). At ⌐236 (**1h05min**), go

The Authion from the Scoubayoun ridge

straight ahead for L'ARPIHA. You come to a second ⬆236 at a grassy COL. From here scramble up to the **Cime de l'Arpiha** (1634m/5360ft; **1h25min**), to enjoy some magnificent views — west to the deeply-etched Planchette and Bollène valleys running towards the Vésubie, and east to the spread of the Authion massif.

Return to the *first* ⬆236 you met on the way up (at the 1h05min-point) and turn left. This path rises 150m/495ft in deep shade to the highest point in the walk, the **Tête de Scoubayoun**, then drops 50m/165ft back to the clearing at spot height 1648. Turn left here, to retrace your steps back to the **Col de Turini** (**2h40min**).

The path to the Tête de Scoubayon in the venerable forest of Turini

Walk 13: LAC DE TRECOLPAS AND REFUGE DE LA COUGOURDE

NB: See notes about the Mercantour National Park on page 73.
See map page 108
Distance: 10km/6.2mi; 4h20min
Grade: moderate-strenuous, with an ascent/descent of 520m/1700ft overall. The first half of the walk (up to Trécolpas Lake) is one long steady pull. Beyond the lake the walk levels out, before descending. Yellow PR, red and white GR waymarking. *IGN map 3741 OT*
Equipment: see page 72; binoculars. Make sure you have enough warm clothing. Refreshments available at Le Boréon
Travel: 🚗 to the 'Parking supérieur du Boréon' (Car tour 2; details pages 21-22). No 🚌 service
Short walk/picnic suggestion: Chalet Vidron. 2.7km/1.7mi; 1h. Easy. Follow the main walk for 30 minutes and return the same way.
Short walk: Le Boréon — Pont de Peïrastrèche — Le Boréon. 4km/2.5mi; 1h55min. Fairly easy ascent/descent of 180m/600ft. Follow the main walk across the **Pont de Peïrastrèche**. At ⚑423 go left on the GR52, descending past the tiered cascade seen earlier. The GR bends left in front of a scree, drops past the Chalet Vidron on the far bank and comes to a Y-fork (30min below the bridge). Go left here, on a wide grassy track, over a bridge. Four minutes later fork left again. In seven minutes, with a restaurant ahead, go left at ⚑419 ('Chalet Vidron', etc). Rise to a crossing track, go left towards the Vachérie du Boréon and pass to the right of it, taking a stony path back up to ⚑420 (**1h55min**).
Alternative walk ***(for very experienced walkers):*** **Le Boréon — Lac de Trécolpas — Pas des Ladres — Madone de Fenestre.** 9km/5.6mi; 5h15min. Strenuous climb of 800m/2625ft, followed by a descent of 550m/1800ft. Arrange for friends/a taxi to collect you at Madone de Fenestre and take you back to your car. Better, walk with friends who also have a car, and leave one car at Madone de Fenestre. Follow the main walk to the **Lac de Trécolpas** and from there continue on the GR52 to the **Pas des Ladres** *(the last part of this climb is a steep, difficult scramble on all fours)*. At the pass pick up Walk 14 at the 2h20min-point, to descend to **Madone de Fenestre**.

This is one of the most rewarding walks in the Mercantour National Park — especially considering the little effort involved. There is ample shade on the lower slopes, and much of the walk follows a foaming stream. But the two highlights are the teal-blue Lac de Trécolpas and the magnificent rock bastion of La Cougourde. Throughout the walk be alert: you will find many pockets of alpine flora and almost certainly see chamois.

The Refuge de la Cougourde (open mid-June until mid-September) is a welcoming sight in cold, changeable weather. Behind it rises one of the best-known motifs of the Mercantour — La Cougourde. Varnished to a golden hue when this picture was taken, the colour has weathered to a faded brown.

Start the walk at at the **Parking supérieur du Boréon**. From |▪420, head east on the stony track behind the barrier (a continuation of the track on which you parked). This climbs gently through the **Vallon du Haut Boréon**. Pass a track off right signposted 'Cime du Pisset' and, at a Y-fork where the track bends right (|▪421), keep straight ahead on a stony path. Soon the summits where we are heading are visible, tinged with chartreuse lichen. Cross a

bridge and arrive at the **Chalet Vidron** (|▪422; **30min**), a stone hut beside a tiny lake. This is a delightful place for a picnic and, in late spring, you will find pockets of violets and gentians nearby. Below the chalet there's more good picnicking on the banks of the roaring stream, just below a lovely tiered cascade and with scree-strewn slopes of Mont Pélago rising on the far side.

From here follow REFUGE DE COUGOURDE, PAS DES LADRES, climbing steeply in zigzags. There are no paint waymarks, but the clear path is easily

followed as you climb through the rocky chaos. Soon the sound of rushing water heralds your arrival at the **Pont de Peïrastrèche (55min)**. Cross the bridge (another pleasant picnic spot) and quickly come to ⌐423. Follow *LAC DE TRECOLPAS, REFUGE DE LA COUGOURDE, PAS DES LADRES*. Now you have joined the GR52 and soon begin climbing in earnest; watch for the red and white flashes as the path keeps hard by the banks of the stream. Ten minutes from the Pont de Peïrastrèche cross a *LOG BRIDGE* over a tributary, and a couple of minutes later cross another attractive *LOG BRIDGE*. You cross a fourth *LOG BRIDGE* **(1h10min)**, and with every step you draw nearer to the magnificent *cirque* before you. Five minutes later a fifth *BRIDGE* is crossed, and another

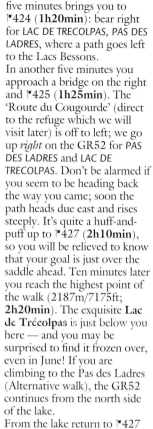

five minutes brings you to ⌐424 **(1h20min)**: bear right for *LAC DE TRECOLPAS, PAS DES LADRES*, where a path goes left to the Lacs Bessons. In another five minutes you approach a bridge on the right and ⌐425 **(1h25min)**. The 'Route du Cougourde' (direct to the refuge which we will visit later) is off to left; we go up *right* on the GR52 for *PAS DES LADRES* and *LAC DE TRECOLPAS*. Don't be alarmed if you seem to be heading back the way you came; soon the path heads due east and rises steeply. It's quite a huff-and-puff up to ⌐427 **(2h10min)**, so you will be relieved to know that your goal is just over the saddle ahead. Ten minutes later you reach the highest point of the walk (2187m/7175ft; **2h20min)**. The exquisite **Lac de Trécolpas** is just below you here — and you may be surprised to find it frozen over, even in June! If you are climbing to the Pas des Ladres (Alternative walk), the GR52 continues from the north side of the lake. From the lake return to ⌐427 and go right for *REFUGE DE LA*

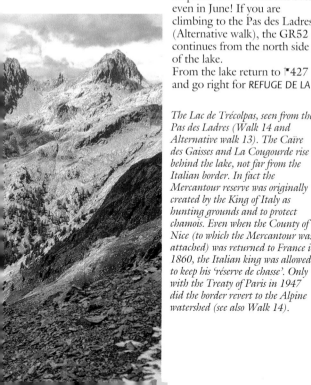

The Lac de Trécolpas, seen from the Pas des Ladres (Walk 14 and Alternative walk 13). The Caïre des Gaisses and La Cougourde rise behind the lake, not far from the Italian border. In fact the Mercantour reserve was originally created by the King of Italy as hunting grounds and to protect chamois. Even when the County of Nice (to which the Mercantour was attached) was returned to France in 1860, the Italian king was allowed to keep his 'réserve de chasse'. Only with the Treaty of Paris in 1947 did the border revert to the Alpine watershed (see also Walk 14).

COUGOURDE. This level path first crosses a gigantic 'scree' of enormous boulders, but later the way is carpeted with soft pine needles. Soon a beacon shines out on the other side of the valley — a gold-varnished mountain hut. A gurgling stream is crossed on a makeshift bridge, and another stream is forded on stepping stones, before you finally reach the **Refuge de la Cougourde (2h50min)**. Idyllically perched beside the rushing stream, the refuge boasts a restaurant (in summer) and even a terrace!

Here ⌐426 points back to the way you've come and to your the trail down to Le Boréon. Walk to the south-facing terrace of the refuge (shown in the photograph on page 106) and you will see your ongoing path. It crosses the stream and

then skirts to the right of it. The good path descends steeply, sometimes on stone steps, and skips over many streams via stepping stones or logs.

Beyond a grassy basin you come back to ⌐425 (**3h20min**). Follow LE BOREON now, to return along your outgoing route. (Just ahead on the left is a water trough where you may see chamois; *go quietly*.) After recrossing the Pont de Peïrastrèche be sure to take the lower path on the right. Descend the clear path through the cairned chaos. Return past the Chalet Vidron to ⌐420 at the **Parking supérieur du Boréon (4h20min)**.

108

Walk 14: COL DE FENESTRE AND PAS DES LADRES

NB: See notes about the Mercantour National Park on page 73.
See map opposite and photographs on pages 8-9 and 106-107
Distance: 8km/5mi; 3h40min
Grade: fairly strenuous, with an ascent/descent of 600m/2000ft. Stony terrain underfoot. Beyond the Col de Fenestre the footpath demands some agility. *No shade.* Red and white GR, yellow PR waymarking. *IGN map 3741 OT*
Equipment: see page 72; binoculars. Make sure you have enough warm clothing. Refreshments available at St-Martin-Vésubie (13km)
Travel: 🚗 to the CAF refuge at Madone de Fenestre (Car tour 2; the road is 200m northwest of St-Martin-Vésubie centre). No 🚌 service
Short walk: Madone de Fenestre — Lac de Fenestre — Madone de Fenestre. 5.5km/3.4mi; 2h. Easy-moderate ascent/descent of 370m/1200ft on a good trail (stout shoes will suffice). Follow the main walk to the lake; return the same way.
Alternative walk: Le Boréon to Madone de Fenestre. See Alternative walk 13, page 105.

This classic walk is steeped in history. It is thought that a Roman temple and travellers' shelter once existed near the spot where the chapel now stands at Madone de Fenestre. But the trail we follow to the Col de Fenestre predates even Roman times. For a thousand years, until the end of World War II, this route was often a battleground. Even in the 16th century, when both sides of the col belonged to the House of Savoy, the breach was closed in a vain effort to stop the plague spreading south from Piedmont to Nice. The detritus of World War II, barbed wire, rubble and bunkhouses, still menaces the Col de Fenestre, which today marks the border with Italy.

Start the walk at **Madone de Fenestre**: climb the steps at the left of the large CAF refuge, to ↑357. Turn right for PAS DES LADRES along the wide, very stony trail (red and white flashes of the GR52). The stream roars away below on the right, beside the Vacherie de la Madone. A splendid *cirque* rises before you, dominated by the summit of Mount Gélas (photograph pages 8-9). At a Y-fork just beyond ↑368 (**25min**), bear right for LAC DE FENESTRE (the GR52, our return route, climbs left here). You quickly ford a stream. Fifteen minutes later a beautiful grassy slope makes a lovely rest stop, from where you look out southeast to the pointed Petit Caïre and the larger Caïre de la Madone. Then trudge on. Your packhorse plodding is rewarded when you reach the glistening **Lac de Fenestre** (**1h05min**), a good place to end the Short walk with a picnic.

Continue ahead towards 2000 years of history, climbing below the needle-sharp heights of the Cime Est de Fenestre. Some 10 minutes beyond the lake, keep right (where a path heads off left towards the crenellated silhouette of Fenestre's western summit (Cime Ouest). You pass below a BUNKER up left, and then a second BUNKER on your right. They were built by the Italians during World War II.

At a crossing path (⌐369; **1h 45min**), go right uphill to the **Col de Fenestre** (2471m/ 8105ft; **1h50min**), where there is another bunker, a cross and a boundary stone. From here a waymarked path continues into Italy. Looking down the wide valley below the Cime du Lombard on the left, it is easy to appreciate why this was a major gateway between France and Italy for thousands of years.

Return to ⌐369 and go straight ahead for *REFUGE DE COUGOURDE, LAC DE TRECOLPAS, PAS DES LADRES*. This narrow path, which requires some agility, offers good views back over the Lac de Fenestre and, on clear days, towards the sparkling Mediterranean. On the final part of the ascent, just when the Lac de Fenestre is out of sight, you head towards the summit of Mount Agnellière, then look northwest to the deep gash of

the Boréon Valley (Walk 13), with Mount Pélago beyond it. When the walk flattens out, a well-engineered path runs through the rocks, and if you look slightly downhill to the west, you will spot the wooden fingerpost at the **Pas des Ladres** (**2h20min**). From here you over look Lake Trécolpas from the vantage point shown on pages 106-107. ⌐428 indicates a path up from the lake (Alternative walk 13) and another path southwest to the Agnellière summit.

Turn left down a narrow path in front of a huge cairn (GR flashes; ⌐: *MADONE DE FENESTRE*). Very quickly, turn back sharp left downhill, where the Agnellière path goes straight on. As you descend, the Lac de Fenestre comes into view again, and the wide trail followed earlier stands out like a highway. After fording a stream on stepping stones, the path levels out and crosses a scree. As you approach the Petit Caïre again, notice the gulley you crossed on the way up, where moss hangs from the rocks like a wispy beard.

Back at ⌐368 (**3h15min**), retrace your steps to **Madone de Fenestre** (**3h40min**).

The sparkling Lac de Fenestre

Walk 15: CIME DU PISSET

NB: *See notes about the Mercantour National Park on page 73.*
Distance: 9km/5.6mi; 3h40min
Grade: fairly strenuous, with an ascent/descent of 580m/1900ft. You must be agile and sure-footed. Little shade. Some green as well as yellow PR waymarking. *IGN map 3741 OT*
Equipment: as Walk 14, page 109
Travel: 🚌 to La Puncha on the road to Madone de Fenestre (Car tour 2; see page 22). No 🚐 service

The contour path along the Plage de l'Agnellière looks deceptively easy, but you may find landslips in the many tributary valleys.

This lovely walk offers a maximum of 'balcony' views for minimum effort compared with other hikes in the Mercantour. From the Cime du Pisset, the Boréon and Madone de Fenestre valleys open out below you.

Start the walk below the **La Puncha** picnic table, on the north side of the road (🏁355). Following CIME DU PISSET, ignore a trail right to Madone de Fenestre (the return route). The path climbs due north up the **Vallon de la Puncha**; zigzags and good shade help you gain 300m/1000ft in height quite quickly. The path then emerges on bare mountain flanks and rises northwest, now climbing less steeply to signpost 🏁429 (2200m/7220ft; **1h45min**) ... but the sign was missing just before press date.

From here it's just short detour west up to the **Cime du Pisset** viewpoint (🏁430; **2h**). Return to 🏁429 and begin to contour southeast along the **Plage de l'Agnellière** on a 'balcony' path above the Vallon de Fenestre (large green waymarks at time of checking, but *do not follow them downhill: keep to the sparse yellow flashes*). You will come across screes at all the stream bed crossings on this traverse, *most* of them stabilised. If you cannot spot any waymarks after crossing the final stream bed, remember that your goal is *not* the buildings at Madone de Fenestre. Your path zigzags down to the road well *before* the deep stream bed and scree separating you from the large CAF refuge. When you meet the road (🏁356; **3h15min**), turn off right and follow the lovely old pilgrims' trail back down to **La Puncha** (**3h40min**).

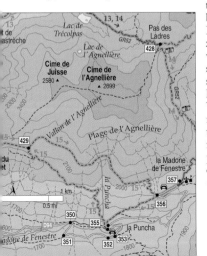

111

Walk 16: CASCADE DE L'ESTRECH

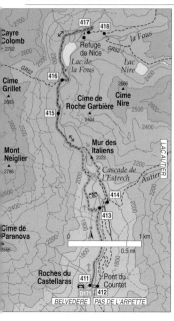

The bounding stream in the upper Gordolasque Valley

NB: *See notes about the Mercantour National Park on page 73.*
Distance: 5.5km/3.4mi; 2h35min
Grade: moderate climb of 340m/1115ft on stony paths; agility required. *No shade.* Yellow PR waymarking. *IGN map 3741 OT*
Equipment: as Walk 14, page 109. Refreshments available at St-Grat (3km) and Belvédère (13km)
Travel: 🚗 to the car park at the end of the road in the Gordolasque Valley (Car tour 2). No 🚌 service
Alternative walk: Refuge de Nice. 11km/6.8mi; 4h. Grade as main walk, with a climb/descent of 540m/1770ft. At the 1h15min-point in the main walk, continue ahead via ▸415 and ▸416 to the **Lac de la Fous** and CAF refuge (refreshments available in summer). Return the same way and pick up the main walk again.
Note: The most famous walk in the Mercantour — to the **Vallée des Merveilles**, where there are more than 30,000 Bronze Age petroglyphs — can be done in a day starting here at the Pont du Countet and climbing via the Pas de l'Arpette to the GR52. This is a day-long, tough walk, and certain areas are only accessible to walkers with an approved guide. To make the most of this hike (some of the engravings are hard to find), you could walk with a guided group: enquire at the tourist office in St-Martin or Belvédère. If you walk on your own, obtain the Park pamphlet showing the restricted areas. *IGN maps 3741 OT, 3841 OT; yellow waymarking*

If you're not doing *the* walk from the Gordolasque (to the Vallée des Merveilles), this short alternative is a delight. It takes you above a gorgeous waterfall, in a setting where you may be tempted to linger all day.

Start out at the CAR PARK: walk through the open barrier, to the walkers' signboards. Don't cross the **Pont du Countet**; take the stony track to the left (⌐: ECOLE D'ESCALADE). Now edge along the stream, in an idyllic setting of cascades and grassy banks. Perhaps the *cirque* ahead will be flecked with snow. Not far beyond the chaos of high boulders used by the climbing school, begin to rise on a

Pont du Countet, where the walk begins

narrow path. Soon the waterfall is seen up ahead. To its right, a rock cliff (Mur des Italiens) seems to close off the valley.

At ☞413 (**25min**) a path goes right, across the river, to Lac Autier and the Mur des Italiens. You will return across this bridge at the end of the walk, but for now swing up left into the first of the hairpin bends on the lower slopes of **Mont Neiglier**. Cairns mark the route where it passes over bedrock. As you reach the final hairpin bend to the left (**1h**), first walk over to the right for a good view of the bounding **Cascade de l'Estreche**. When the path levels out (**1h10min**), you will see another path on the far side of the river, below the Mur des Italiens. Soon you can cross the steam on

STEPPING STONES (**1h15min**) to join it. *(But for the Alternative walk, keep straight ahead.)*

Now heading back south below the 'Italians' Wall', you walk through the walls of a RUINED FORTIFICATION and later pass a massive CAIRN, overlooking a beautiful teal-blue RIVER POOL (**1h45min**). At ☞414 (**1h55min**), ignore the earthen path climbing ahead to Lac Autier; go right downhill on the wider stony path, towards the river. On reaching the old electricity workers' road (☞413; just over **2h**), head down steps, cross the **Gordolasque Stream** on the bridge you spotted earlier, and retrace your outgoing route back to the **Pont du Countet** and CAR PARK (**2h35min**).

The hamlet of St-Grat, backed by the cirque *at the head of the valley*

Walk 17: CIRCUIT FROM GOURDON

Distance: 9km/5.6mi; 3h
Grade: fairly easy, with a steep, very stony descent of 200m/650ft at the start and a gradual ascent of under 300m/1000ft near the end. Red and white GR, yellow PR way-marking. *IGN map 3643 ET*
Equipment: see page 72; binoculars; a *torch is essential.* Refreshments available at Gourdon
Travel: 🚌 (Car tour 3, page 28) or 🚌 512 from Grasse (www.departement06.fr/vous-deplacer-en-bus/lignes-et-horaires-3029.html) to Gourdon

Alternative walk: Gourdon — Le Bar-sur-Loup.
4km/2.5mi; 2h. Fairly easy, but initially steep and stony, descent of 450m/1475ft; no torch needed. Yellow waymarks. At the 30min-point in the main walk cross over the **Aqueduc du Foulon** and keep descending until you come to the **Aqueduc du Loup**, where you turn right. After 25 minutes along this level path turn left downhill (📷: LE BAR). A stone-laid trail takes you to

the **Chapelle St-Claude**. Walk alongside the CEMETERY, then follow the Chemin de la Bessurane and Rue du Ribas to the centre (photograph page 27). Return to Gourdon by taxi (11km) or climb back the same way (2h30min). If scheduling permits, you can also take 🚌 511 from here to Grasse and then 🚌 512 back to Gourdon (website as above).

The first part of this walk, a descent on the aptly-named 'Paradise Trail', is an extravaganza of bird's-eye views down over the lush Loup Valley and the coast. We then follow a piped watercourse through aromatic pines, in the company of butterflies and dark red squirrels. At the end of the walk, there is a gradual climb under the pleasant shade of oaks.

Start out at the CAR PARK/BUS STOP below **Gourdon**; walk up towards the castle, but fork left down stone steps to the WC (before the village centre). Past the WC, at the end of the path, more steps take you down into the **Gourdon Valley** on an old mule trail, the **Chemin du Paradis**. In five minutes, you

come to a wide ledge, a superb picnic spot overlooking the coast. The Montagne de Cour-mettes rises on the far side of the Loup Gorge (where you may spot paragliders). Notice the piers of the old viaduct, destroyed in World War II, and the large water pipe below — your ongoing route.

When you meet the fat old rusty pipe (**Aqueduc du Foulon**; **30min**), turn right alongside it (⊩: GRASSE). *(The Alternative walk continues straight ahead downhill here.)* You will follow this pipe, in the company of the red and white flashes of the GR51, for just under an hour (keep your torch handy for the tunnels).

Whenever there is a break in the trees, you enjoy a fine outlook over the coast (the wedge-shaped apartments at Baie des Anges can serve as a landmark: they are just west of Cagnes and east of Antibes). A particularly fine outlook comes up just as the aqueduct rounds a bend: you have a perfect view down over Le Bar

Gourdon rises some 600m/2000ft above the Loup. The Chemin du Paradis, an old mule trail, zigzags from the château down the steep mountainside. On the descent your view stretches from Cap Ferrat in the east to Nice, the mouth of the Var, Antibes and its cape, the Lérin Islands, Cannes and its observatory, the Maures, and the relays on Pic de l'Ours and Mont Vinaigre in the Esterel.

and along the whole sweep of coast from the hills behind Eze to the Maures. Now, as you head west, the path rounds an steep escarpment, protected by railings.

On coming to a 'crossroads' (**1h25min**), turn right up a steep concreted lane. On your left, olive groves grace a deep basin. Four minutes later, ignore the left fork back to the canal; follow the GR uphill to the right, on the concrete lane. But six minutes later, when the GR heads off to the left, keep *straight ahead* on a tarmac lane (☛: BOIS DE GOURDON). After another five minutes turn left off this lane: go up STEPS (☛: BOIS DE GOURDON; **1h40min**). Now *carefully* follow the yellow waymarks along a narrow path through oaks and spring-flowering broom. Almost immediately you come to a T-junction of small paths; both are waymarked, but turn *right* here.

When you come to a crossing cart track (**1h50min**), follow it to the left (MAGENTA ARROW). After several paces, another track curves in front of you at a T-junction: turn left here. You pass a huge PIT in half a minute and then cross straight over the D3 (**1h53min**). On the far side of the road, take the path straight ahead (yellow flash on a tree) that joins a gravel track near a CISTERN.

Five minutes later, be sure to turn off this fire-break track, going left on a stony trail (posts with magenta waymarks at the outset). As you climb this lovely woodland trail, ignore two paths off left (after one minute and four minutes later). Soon look right through the trees: you are level with

Gourdon on the far side of the valley. This woodland was once the hunting grounds of the Counts of Gourdon … and the scene of violent clashes between the inhabitants of Gourdon and Le Bar, both of whom claimed the right to collect its wood.

On coming to a strong crossing stony trail (**2h15min**), *go straight over,* even if you don't spot any waymarks ahead. Five minutes later cross straight over the fire-break onto a path. After another five minutes an old stone-laid trail comes in from the left; continue to the right, straight towards the Loup Gorge. In a minute you join a good gravel track: turn right. Now the walk, again in full sun, descends gradually across a plateau, with more spectacular views — to Gourdon, the Loup cleft and the coast. You pass a CROSS on the left near a QUARRY and then cross a BRIDGE. Tarmac comes under foot: turn right here and follow this lane for about 800m/yds to the D12. Then head right, back to the CAR PARK (**3h**).

Now visit well-restored **Gourdon**, not missing the *table d'orientation* behind the church. The 13/14th-century castle, built on the foundations of a Saracen fortress, houses a history museum and a gallery of naïve art. If you are unable to resist all the craft shops, at least you won't have to lug all your souvenirs round the Loup Valley!

Walk 18: CASTELLARAS

Distance: 3km/2mi; 1h30min
Grade: fairly easy climb and descent of 245m/800ft, but the paths are quite stony. Yellow PR waymarking. *IGN map 3542 ET*
Equipment: see page 72;

refreshments available at Thorenc (2km)
Travel: 🚗 to a small parking area on the D2 (0.6km west of the junction with the D5, at ↑145; Car tours 3, 4). No 🚐 service

East of Thorenc, between the Lane and Loup valleys, an impressive plinth of rock rises above the D2, crowned by the remains of a 12th-century castle. The site dominates one of the finest panoramas in the Grasse Pre-Alps, and it is probable that a Ligurian *oppidum* existed here as early as 600BC.

Start out at ↑145; follow the track running south, rising through box and stunted pines gnarled into whimsical 'bonsai'

shapes. Soon a huge doorway appears in the crest above. At a fork (**12min**), go right — you'll spot a yellow waymark a couple of minutes later. Ignore a stony path down left to the D5 (**20min**); turn sharp right. Five minutes later, at a grassy *SADDLE* strewn with wild flowers, you come upon ↑146, where another path leads south to the D5. Climb up left to the **Castellaras** (**50min**), passing through its 2ft-thick drystone walls. Explore the château, towers, and vaulted chapel. Then take in the vast panorama. Bauroux (Walk 22) rises in the west, the Col de Bleine with its relay in the north and Cheiron in the northeast. In the south the Audibergue dominates the Loup Valley, which can be traced southeast to its gorge and the Col de Vence.
Then retrace your steps to ↑145 (**1h30min**).

Walk 19: SOURCE DE LA SIAGNOLE

Distance: 10.5km/6.5mi; 2h25min

Grade: easy ascent/descent of under 100m/330ft overall, but requiring some agility on narrow paths. Some red and white GR waymarking. *IGN map 3543 ET*

Equipment: see page 72 (trainers will suffice); refreshments available at Mons (7km)

Travel: 🚗 to the bridge over the Siagnole at Les Moulins (D56, 6.8km south of the parking area in Mons; Car tour 4). No 🚌 service

Short walks

1 Chapelle St-Peire. 4.5km/ 2.8mi; 1h20min. Easy. Follow the main walk for 40min and return the same way.

2 Source de la Siagnole. 2km/1.2mi; 50min. Easy. Walk to the sign *LA SIAGNOLE* on the south side of the bridge and turn right just beyond it, climbing a steep, sometimes mucky path. At a fork two-three minutes uphill, go left. In a minute or two you meet a major footpath (by some FLUORESCENT RED WAYMARKS); turn right. This sometimes narrow path (watch your

footing) covers the old ROMAN AQUEDUCT; at one point you will have to squat down under a rock overhang. Go through a first BARRIER (barring motor-bikes) and walk ahead past a second barrier, to the left of a SHELTER; then keep ahead to the fenced-in **Source de la Siagnole** (25min). If you wish to picnic, refer to the main walk notes at the 1h50min-point. Return the same way.

Thus beautiful walk above the gorges of the Siagnole, mostly in the shade of oaks, is perfect for a hot day. Before setting off, visit the *table d'orientation* in Mons, to identify all the landmarks in the area.

Start out at Les Moulins. Cross the bridge over the **Siagnole** and walk south along the D56 for 500m/yds, then turn left off the road on a path. Some agility is needed here, and there may be a 'Danger' sign. Many walkers still use this path, which used to be the GR route (the GR now follows the road). Soon you're walking through the rock passage shown overleaf (**Roche**

Taillée; **12min**), hewn out by the Romans to accommodate a watercourse. Continue along the earthen path atop the aqueduct, in the shade of oaks.

When a path heads uphill to the right (under **20min**), *keep ahead* (it is the *return* route). Four minutes later ignore another path off to the right. Breaks in the foliage permit fine views over to Mons and

119

down the gorge towards
St-Cézaire, setting for Walk
21. Eventually (**35min**) the
path swings away from the
Siagnole and you join a grassy
track. Keep straight ahead.
Two minutes later, on coming
to a T-junction with an earthen
track, turn left. Almost immediately, you walk through an
opening in a stone wall, past a
WINDMILL on your right, and
come to the tiny **Chapelle
St-Peire** (**40min**). Although

we've never seen anyone here, both the mill and the chapel stand on private property, so please do not linger.

Return to the T-junction and go straight on (west), following electricity lines and ignoring tracks to the left and then right. When you reach a Y-fork (**55min**), bear right to the D37, and turn right. Walk ahead to a sign indicating a crossroads and, 75m/yds beyond the sign, turn right on a footpath, crushing wild herbs underfoot as you go. This short-cut path takes you to the D56, where you turn right for 20 paces and then turn right on a footpath (again, this was the old GR route and you may well see old red/white waymarks). Descending through *garrigues,* the pretty path affords fine views over to the bald summits of the Audibergue.

When the path drops you back down to the AQUEDUCT at the point first passed 20min into the walk (**1h10min**), turn *sharp left.* (Straight ahead leads back to the St-Peire chapel.) Retrace your outgoing route back through the **Roche Taillée** to the D56 (**1h 20min**). Cross the road and continue along the lovely shady path. You are still atop the aqueduct. Ignore all paths and trails to the left and right. Soon the Siagnole makes its presence felt, burbling along on your right, in the shadow of the Val-bouissole cliffs. Pass through a first BARRIER (**1h45min**) and shortly, a second BARRIER, by a concrete HUT. The path ends in front of the fenced-off **Source de la Siagnole** (**1h50min**).

To reach the source (and a lovely picnic place), return to the BARRIER WITH THE HUT and turn left downhill on a steep and slippery trail just beyond it. This takes you to a FORD which is easily crossed *(unless the stream is running high).** Turn left on the cart track on the far side, to a stand of very tall oaks and a circle of boulder 'seats'. Nearby is the SOURCE itself, behind a small metal gate bearing the date 1918.

From here retrace your steps past the BARRIER WITH THE HUT to the next BARRIER, then turn left at the Y-fork of paths (you descended the path to the right here). You are now on the lower aqueduct and the path is just as attractive, cool with moss and ivy and the sound of the river tinkling beside you on the left. Five minutes along, when the aqueduct rounds a steep escarpment, railings protect the drop to the left, but you have to squat down under an overhang of rock, chiselled out by the Romans. *Watch your footing.*

Six minutes past the railings, turn left down a steep, mucky path, following FLUORESCENT RED WAYMARKS. Below, through the trees, you can see Les Moulins. Ignore the path down left three minutes into the descent (it goes to the mill); keep straight ahead. A minute later you meet the D56: turn left, back to the BRIDGE at **Les Moulins** (**2h25min**).

---

*There is also a footbridge just downstream from this ford, but it is gated and often *locked;* if you returned from the picnic area to find the bridge locked, you would have to follow the cart track via Les Gombauds back to the D56 (see map.)

Walk 20: GORGES DU BLAVET

See photograph page 32
Distance: 7.5km/4.7mi; 2h
Grade: easy descent/ascent of 170m/560ft. Yellow PR, red and white GR waymarking. *IGN map 3544 ET*
Equipment: see page 72; refreshments available at Bagnols
Travel: Approaching Bagnols on the D47 (Car tour 4), watch for the Chapelle Notre-Dame on your right, just before the wine co-op. Turn right here; after 100m go right again on the Chemin de Bayonne. Park at the Castel de Bayonne, 1.7km beyond a TV mast. No 🚐 service
Extension: See violet highlighting and alternative parking. *NB:* the river must be forded twice on slippery stones.

This walk is memorable for its fine views of the red-rock cliffs shown on page 32, the sweetly-scented *maquis,* and the pretty rock pools in the Gorges du Blavet. On fine days you'll also have a splendid outlook to the Rocher de Roquebrune rising in the south.

Start out at the **Castel de Bayonne**: walk back downhill (the way you came). A few metres/yards below the estate's fencing, turn *sharp* left down a narrow path (YELLOW FLASH). Descend gently through typical *maquis,* before the landscape opens out to give fine views west to the Colle Rousse (**20min**). Later the Bayonne summit (ancient oppidum) rises on the left.
Meeting a stony crossing trail (**Piste de Bayonne; 33min**), turn right (left is your return route). Then turn left at a WATER TANK on a stony trail (☞: GORGES DU BLAVET). Soon the Colle Rousse rises in the background. Go left at a Y-fork (the way to the right *may* be marked with an 'X'). Then you meet a wide crossing path waymarked in the red and white flashes of the GR51 (**45min**). Follow it to the left downhill, descending to the RIVER POOLS in the **Gorges du Blavet** (**50min**). From here the GR will ford the river — a splendid extension, crossing twice on slippery STEPPING STONES and once on a BRIDGE and passing a gigantic CAVE (☞).
But for the less agile it is easier to retrace steps from here to the WATER TANK (**1h10min**) and turn right on the stony trail. Rise past the path you descended earlier. Ignore a path off left to the Bayonne summit (**1h25min**), then take a break at the beautiful outcrop of red rock on the right — looking out to the gorges and the massive Rocher de Roquebrune on the far side of the Argens Valley.
Five minutes past this viewpoint keep left at a fork (GR WAYMARKS). Keep following GR WAYMARKS, past another WATER TANK on the right (**1h50min**) and fields full of autumn-flowering heather, all the way back to the **Castel de Bayonne** (**2h**).

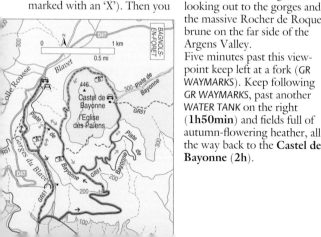

Walk 21: GORGES DE LA SIAGNE

See also photograph page 31
Distance: 9.5km/6mi; 3h
Grade: moderate-strenuous,
with descents/ascents of 440m/
1445ft overall. Some of the
stony paths require agility.
Yellow PR, red/white GR waymarking. *IGN map 3543 ET*
Equipment: see page 72;
swimming things. Refresh-
ments available at St-Cézaire
Travel: 🚍 33 from Grasse
(www.sillages.eu) to
St-Cézaire-sur-Siagne or 🚗
(Car tour 4); park at the
'Chapelle Romane' (N-D de
Sardaigne), south of the D13,
on the southeast side of the
village.

**Alternative walk: Pont des
Tuves and Pont des Moulins.**
8km/5mi; 2h45min. Moderate,
with a descent and re-ascent of
310m/1015ft requiring agility.
Follow the main walk to ▸7
and turn right on the short-cut
path. Zigzag down to ▸8,
where you join the GR510.
Turn right to ▸9 and descend
(crossing the **Canal de la
Siagne**) to the **Pont des
Tuves**. Cross the bridge and
turn right on a yellow-
waymarked path. This
undulates above the river,
passing the ruins of the **Tour
de Siagne** and then a paper
mill. Cross the **Pont des
Moulins** and, on the far side,
rise up to the canal again. Now
you have a choice: *either*
continue ahead (yellow

waymarks) on the old road
between St-Cézaire and Callian
or turn right along the canal
and follow it back to the
yellow-waymarked descent
path to the Pont des Tuves,
climb up to the GR (7min)
and turn left back to
St-Cézaire. *The second option is
always our choice,* but you must
reckon on an *additional*
3km/2mi; 45min.
Note: This is just one of *many*
walks around St-Cézaire. The
excellent tourist office should
be able to advise about others.

Almost all walks from St-Cézaire eventually cross the
Canal de la Siagne … and that's a big problem for
us! We're so distracted and enchanted by this beautiful
watercourse that we abandon all plans for a 'proper'
walk and end up just following the canal. If you love
the canals of Provence as much as we do, then be sure
to pack a torch, so you can follow this one for as long
as you like.

overlook the **Siagne Valley**, where a wonderful view opens up northwest along the gorge. At a fork 700m/yds along, keep right downhill, past beautiful houses set in terraced olive groves.

At ↑3 (**20min**), keep right on the forestry track. Almost immediately, at another fork (↑7), keep left. *(But for the Alternative walk, take the path to the right, which zigzags straight down to the canal.)* You soon leave the track, to take a path on the right, continuing more or less in the same direction. Ignoring a wide path to the left signposted to Tuves, zigzag fairly steeply downhill, crossing the **Canal de la Siagne**, to ↑6, where you join the GR510. Follow the GR to the left for 200m/yds; then, at ↑5, descend to the **Chapelle Saint-Saturnin** (**1h**).

Return to ↑6 and now follow the GR up the valley, recrossing the canal. At ↑8 the short-cut path from ↑7 comes in from the right. At ↑9, keep left downhill, leaving the GR and following yellow waymarks. You cross the canal yet again and descend to the beautiful **Pont des Tuves** (**1h45min**).

After taking a break in this lovely setting, return to ↑9 and turn left for *ST-CEZAIRE*. This old donkey trail doesn't offer much shade, and although it's beautifully graded, it still takes almost an hour to rise up to the centre of **St-Cézaire** (**3h**). Wander around the lovely village, take in the view from the *table d'orientation* and then return to the **Chapelle N-D de Sardaigne**.

The walk begins at the lovely Romanesque **Chapelle N-D de Sardaigne** in **St-Cézaire**. Take the lane on the south side of the building (↑1), the **Chemin des Puits de Chautard**. After 500m/yds (at ↑2), turn right on another lane, the **Chemin du Courbon**. Descending between stone walls, you

Walk 22: SERANON AND THE BAUROUX RIDGE

See also photographs on pages 1 and 29

Distance: 13km/8mi; 4h45min

Grade: quite strenuous, with ascents/descents of 650m/ 2130ft overall. The descent path requires agility and *confidence;* less experienced walkers should retrace their steps from the summit. Red and white GR, yellow PR way-marking. *IGN map 3542 ET*

Equipment: see page 72; walking stick(s). Refreshments available at Séranon and Caille

Travel: 🚗 to Séranon (Car tour 4; park in the square) or 🚐 800 from Grasse (www.sillages.eu)

Short walks: All are easy and take under 2h. 1) follow the main walk to **Vieux Séranon** and back; 2) climb from **N-D-de-Gratemoine** to the **Chapelle Ste-Brigitte** or to **Vieux Séranon** and return via the Séranon cemeteries (🚐 800 or

The Route Napoléon from Vieux Séranon

🚗 to N-D-de-Gratemoine on the D6085; then see lilac line on the map); 3) take the beautiful cart track from **Caille** to **Séranon** and back; access by 🚗 or 🚐 800 (as above) to Caille, then pick up the main walk at the 4h15min-point).

Of all the landscapes in the south of France, one of the most magical for us is the chapel of Notre-Dame-de-Gratemoine on the Route Napoléon below Séranon (see photograph on page 29). How many times we've picnicked there, looking up at the magnificent crest of Bauroux! This long walk leads you gently to the tremendous summit viewpoint and then drops you (literally) back down to Caille's grassy valley.

At the Bauroux summit, where there is now a cross

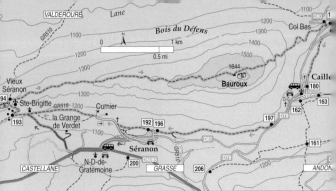

The walk begins in the village square in **Séranon**: follow GR waymarks to the north side of the village and ☞192 *(RUINES DU VIEUX SERANON).* Ignoring the lane, take the grassy path uphill here, just to the right of some houses. Pass some ruins on the left, then join a cart track and continue in the same direction. When you come to the *CEMETERY,* turn right, keeping the cemetery to your left. Join a road and follow it uphill to the right, passing above the *OLD CEMETERY* below on the left. When the lane curls right up to the hamlet of **Curnier**, keep left on a path (☞: *CHAPELLE STE-BRIGITTE*). One minute later, at a Y-fork,

you can either take the grassy cart track on the right or the GR path at the left. They rejoin just before the **Chapelle Ste-Brigitte** (**45min**), a fine place for a break.

Beyond the chapel keep ahead for *BAUROUX* (☞193). Three minutes from the signpost you come to the first ruins of **Vieux Séranon**. The path passes to the left of the huge buttressed church and continues steeply uphill to the *TOP OF THE LONG BAUROUX RIDGE* (**1h**).

Follow the path straight ahead towards *VALDEROURE,* but leave it (*and* the GR) a minute later at ☞194: turn right for *BAUROUX,* now following yellow PR waymarks. This

path, just below the north side of the crest, rises slowly for well over 3km through the thickly-wooded **Bois du Défens**, affording only brief glimpses down into the Lane Valley. It's a long way to go without views, but the mossy path, with soft pine needles underfoot is cool and pleasant. *Finally* you spot the cross ahead, marking the SUMMIT OF **Bauroux** (1644m/5392ft; **2h45min**). Fling yourself down in the golden grass and absorb the 360° panorama: to the east you look down over the green, green plains shown in the photograph below; to the east you can see the Esterel, to the west the Verdon, and to the north the Esteron.

After your break the real fun begins. The path down the northeast side of the mountain is marked with yellow flashes (and, later, plastic tags on rocks). Wait till you see the postage-stamp village of Caille straight below you from the edge of the ridge! Soon the path just drops through a rock chaos, where you'll spend a lot

of time on all fours (and probably searching in vain for waymarks). Just keep down, down, and you will come back to the main path, which eventually descends gently below pines. When you come to two WATER TANKS, circle half-way round them, then turn sharp right down a cart track.

Meeting the D80 at **Col Bas** (**4h**), turn left to ⌐181 and there go right on a track towards CAILLE. Just before a property, curl left, down towards the D79. Turn right on this road and, after 150m/yds, turn left on a concrete drive. At a Y-fork, keep left on a cart track which passes to the left of a house. *Before* reaching the house, go left down a path. It widens to a lane and you pass to the left of the CEMETERY walls and rise to ⌐180 in **Caille**. Take steps on the right up to a road and turn left. Then turn right uphill in front of the MAIRIE, and pass to the left of the CHURCH and to the right of ⌐162. Keep ahead to a junction, join the D79 and follow it straight ahead, past the POST OFFICE on the right (**4h15min**). (This is where you start the walk if you come by bus.) Pass an IRON CROSS on your right and, 300m/yds further on (at ⌐197), take a cart track on the right. All the forks along this track are well waymarked. The trail descends gently amid the lush valley scenery, to **Séranon** (**4h45min**).

View from the Bauroux summit down over the Lane (left) and Loup valleys; the Montagne de l'Hubac separates the two.

Walk 23: LAC D'ALLOS

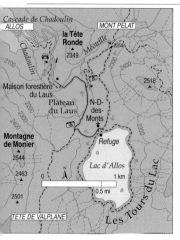

NB: *See notes about the Mercantour National Park on page 73.*

See also photographs on page 36

Distance: 8km/5mi; 2h35min

Grade: easy ascent/descent of 200m/650ft. Yellow/green PR waymarking. *IGN map 3540 ET*

Equipment: see page 72; swimming things; warm clothing in cold weather.

Refreshments: at Allos or the lake (in high season)

Travel: 🚌 to the Lac d'Allos (paying) car park on the Plateau du Laus (Car tour 5). The road is only open to cars from 15 June to 15 October — outside this period, you will have to park 5km lower down, at the car park for the Cascade de Valplane, adding a good 300m/1000ft of ascent/descent (1h30min up, 1h10min back down); there are some signposted short-cuts via the GR56B, which eventually rejoins the road to the upper parking. No 🚐 service

Short walk: Lac d'Allos. 5.5km/3.4mi; 1h50min. Grade as main walk. Follow the main walk, but omit the circuit of the lake.

Alternative walks: At the web page www.valdallos.com/maps.html you will find a 'Rambles Map' which can be downloaded. The whole site has an English version with plenty of information.

Beautifully laid out as a nature trail, this walk in the most westerly valley of the Mercantour National Park is a fascinating introduction to Alpine geology. But *don't* just follow everyone else straight to the lake; first come with us to a high plateau of breathtaking beauty — where, in summer, you are guaranteed to see bushy-tailed marmots galore.

Start out at the LAUS/LAC D'ALLOS CAR PARK: follow the stony path (🏷: LAC D'ALLOS) up past a FORESTRY HOUSE. The **Chadoulin Stream** rushes by on the right. Beyond a WILLOW GROVE, planted to prevent erosion of the stream banks, you cross a tributary, the **Méouille**, and join a track. Soon an information panel calls your attention to some lichen-encrusted rocks (**15min**). A minute later, turn sharp left up a path (🏷: MONT PELAT). (The track, your return route, continues ahead to the lake.) This shady path climbs quickly above the Ravin de Méouille down to the left, and you come upon a gorgeous amphitheatre — a meadow surrounded by high mountains, guaranteed to impart that fantastic 'top-of-the-world' feeling. On a hot day there is ample shade for picnicking here; on a cool day it's a sun trap. If you look right, you can see the Tours du Lac on the far side of the Lac d'Allos. Walk across the meadow, straight towards the pyramids of the Trou de l'Aigle and Mont Pélat (photograph page 36).

On reaching a signpost (spot height 2259m; **40min**), turn sharp right for LAC D'ALLOS, ignoring a path left to Mount Pélat and another half right to the Col de la Cayolle. When the grassy path approaches a ROCK CHAOS WITH A SHEEP-FOLD, follow the yellow and green waymarks carefully: you must keep this *moraine* (boulders plucked up and deposited by the glacier) *to your left*. Soon you enjoy a first glimpse of the lake below the rock 'towers' but, before rushing down to it, visit the drystone chapel, **Notre-Dame-des-Monts** (**1h05min**).

Then descend to the refuge/ restaurant (open end June to early September) and from here amble round the lake. After you've circled this sparkling blue mirror (**1h50min**), climb the wide

Notre-Dame-des-Monts

track from the refuge, past huge stalks of summer-flowering mullein. Beyond a path off left to the Tête de Valplane, you come to a *table d'orientation* looking out towards the mountains and explaining their Alpine vegetation. But don't miss the wonderful view down to the left, where the Chadoulin Stream (a resurgence of the Lac d'Allos) threads delicate meanders through the emerald cushions of the **Plateau du Laus**, the spongy peat bog

At the start of the walk, willows mark the crossing of the Méouille stream — and provide an opportunity to extoll the benefits of aspirin.

shown on page 36. The plateau was once a shallow lake, formed by the same glacier as Lake Allos.

From here you descend through larch woods *(mélèze)*. These clever conifers, 'Kings of the Alps', shed their leaves in winter, an so are less susceptible to damp and cold. Notice how gracefully they curve, as light and gravity influence their growth. Back at the FORESTRY HOUSE above the CAR PARK (**2h35min**), you cross bedrock *(verrou)* — stone so hard that it resisted glacial erosion.

Perhaps now, like us, you'll spend the rest of the day beside the meanders of the Chadoulin, while the crowds hurry past on their way to the lake.

Lac d'Allos

Walk 24: ABOVE BEUIL

Distance: 8km/5mi; 2h45min
Grade: easy-moderate, with ascents/descents of 320m/1050ft overall. Little shade. Yellow PR waymarking; some short pathless sections are marked with wooden sighting posts. *IGN map 3640 OT*
Equipment: see page 72; refreshments available at Beuil
Travel: 🚗 to Beuil (Car tour 6; park at the tourist office on the main D28 road) or 🚌 700 from Nice to Beuil (www.departement06.fr/ vous-deplacer-en-bus/lignes-et-horaires-3029.html); alight at the tourist office
Short walk: Rétouria. 4.5km/2.8mi; 1h25min. Easy ascent/descent of 60m/200ft. Follow

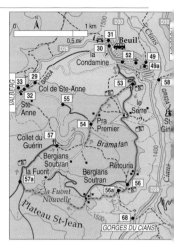

the main walk to **Rétouria** and return the same way.

While we whizz through the eyesore of Valberg trying not to look left or right, Beuil stops us in our tracks. Its setting is just stunning. There are several walks around this Alpine village, but we're convinced that this circuit shows it off to best advantage, whatever the season.

Start out at the TOURIST OFFICE on the main road (D28) in **Beuil**. Walk down the road towards GORGES DU CIANS. Some 300m/yds downhill, at ⌐52, fork right for CIRCUIT DE BRAMAFAN. Fork left 50m/yds along. The track soon rises in zigzags, to a SHRINE on the right (⌐53; **15min**). Continue straight ahead at this junction, ignoring the cart track to the right (the return route). Rising gently on the northeastern flanks of the **Plateau St-Jean**, you have fine views back to Beuil and down left into the **Cians Valley**, with the little St-Ginié chapel on the far bank.

At a Y-fork by some buildings (just past the shrine), keep left, on the main track. Beyond the little hamlet of **Le Serre**

All the little hamlets are beautifully kept. In autumn the wayside is decorated with blooms — seemingly just for the pleasure of walkers!

(**25min**), you cross a stream. Beuil disappears from view, but Les Cluots (2106m/ 6907ft) in the southeast now attracts your attention: its summit is almost always snow-capped. **Rétouria** (**45min**) is another pretty little hamlet, with wooden-roofed stone houses. From here you have a good view down south towards the Cians Gorge.

At ⊩56 you come upon another handful of houses. Go *left* here, for CIANS, leaving the 'Bramafan' circuit and zigzagging down towards the road in the Cians Gorge. When you reach ⊩56a (**55min**) some 60m/200ft downhill, turn right at the Y-fork towards BERGIANS SOUBRAN. This narrow and slightly overgrown (but well waymarked) path gently regains the height lost, as it

rises to another group of houses and a wooden ⊩: *ITINERAIRE PEDESTRE*. Here you come to a Y-fork at a BARN in the middle of the hamlet (**1h10min**). Both routes are waymarked, but take the fork to the *left* of the barn and walk down the overgrown path to the stream bed. Rise from the bed for about a minute, then take a faint, *unmarked* path to the right. After 10m/yds the path is clear, and there are yellow flashes on the trees. Soon the path contours above fields, before coming into a patch of forest and then climbing gently through a stream bed wilderness.

At the **Fuont Nouvelle** (**1h25min**) a cart track comes in from the right. Continue to the left of this well on a stony path, still rising up the stream bed. At a fork three minutes

dogs! At the **Collet du Guérin** (**1h55min**), where there is a CROSS on the left and ⌐57 on the right, keep straight ahead on a lane, passing a little turning circle on the right. At a T-junction, turn right on another lane, slightly uphill. The landscape is a blanket of golden grass interwoven with strands of firs and spruce. Seven minutes from the col, after the lane has described a wide curve to the right, watch for a SIGHTING POST on the left and go left down a wide grassy path at the left edge of the woods. It drops straight down to a grassy track and ⌐54 (**2h 10min**). Go half-right here, again following the CIRCUIT DE BRAMAFAN and passing between two cottages at **Pra Premier**. At a Y-fork, keep left downhill, straight towards Beuil. Soon the trail peters out, but just keep steeply downhill through the grassy field, towards a METAL POLE with a yellow flash. There is a beautiful view over the green valley of **La Condamine** and to Beuil. More sighting posts lead you onto a cart track descending from the right. Follow this downhill to the left, to a huge CAIRN. Continue downhill at the left of the cairn, on an old trail, with the remains of stone walls on either side. This brings you back to the SHRINE first passed at the 15min-point (**2h25min**). Turn left and retrace your outward route to **Beuil** (**2h45min**).

along, go right uphill, now climbing a bit more steeply. You pass to the left of a CONCRETE PLINTH (take either path at the fork here). Then walk to the left of a wooden SIGHTING POST, making for the top of the ridge ahead, where the next sighting post is visible (no waymarks).

Having risen to a crossing track, follow it to the right, to ⌐57a (**1h42min**). From here head northeast towards BERGIANS SOUBRAN, crossing a grassy PLATEAU, with a 'top of the world' feeling. Giant thistles and thousands of sheep accompany you, as well as views north to the jagged peaks of the high Mercantour. The hamlet of La Fuont is below to the right. Nearing **Bergians Soubran** you'll surely encounter goats, sheep, geese, hens, cows, horses, cats and

Walk 25: ABOVE PUGET-THENIERS

See also photograph page 173
Distance: 4.5km/2.8mi; 2h
Grade: moderate climb/descent of 330m/1100ft, but you must be sure-footed and have a head for heights. Avoid the walk in mist, strong winds and wet weather. Some of the paths cross *robines* (see page 173), where *care is needed*. Yellow PR waymarking. *IGN map 3641 OT*
Equipment: see page 72; walking stick(s). Refreshments available at Puget-Théniers
Travel: 🚗 (car tour 6) or 🚌 790 (www.departement06.fr/vous-deplacer-en-bus/lignes-et-horaires-3029.html) to the railway station at Puget-Théniers, or 🚂 to Puget-Théniers (Train des Pignes; see page 168; www.trainprovence.com)
Alternative walk: Crête d'Aurafort. 12km/7.4mi; 5h. Grade as main walk, but this is strenuous, with an ascent/descent of 650m/2130ft, *and vertiginous*. Start out 400m/yds west of the railway station, at

▐160 on the north side of the D6202. Follow the red/white waymarked GR510 to ▐161 and ▐162. Turn left on the road here for 50m/yds, then head right, uphill. Soon you begin an exhilarating scramble *in full sun* up the **Castagnet Cliffs** (although not as thrilling as the *via ferrata* which briefly joins the GR between signposts 162b and 164). *Watch for your GR waymarks!* Once on the **Crête d'Aurafort** (photographs overleaf and page 173), continue to the Col de Vélacs (▐167), where you'll see an ancient boundary marker with the French fleur de lys and the Cross of Savoy. Perhaps go a little further, to the Plateau de la Condamine, with its junipers, mushrooms galore, and grazing horses. (There *are* local waymarks all the way to Entrevaux, but in recent years we have found the route far too dangerous, with crumbling *robines*.) Return the same way, descending the Castagnet Cliffs with care.

On the path above Puget-Théniers in autumn

This walk is a good introduction to the *robines* of Haute-Provence. Ranging in colour from off-white to black, they have an austere beauty. Once your boots have 'got to grips' with these deeply-eroded limey-clay slopes, then return another day and do the Alternative walk. You've got to be very fit, but it is *spectacular!* Leaving the olive groves behind, you scale the sheer cliffs behind Puget-Théniers. At the top, a grassy path takes you through holm oaks to the awesome *robines* of the Crête d'Aurafort. And a bonus: *both* walks afford superb long-range views along the orchard valley of the Var.

Start out at the RAILWAY STATION at **Puget-Théniers**, after first calling at the superb tourist office. Walk into the village centre, then take steps at the right of the POST OFFICE up to the **Rue de la Roudoule** and follow it to the CEMETERY (⌐174; **15min**). From the signpost follow a path uphill, cross the road into the cemetery, and continue to the left of the telephone exchange (with the word JUDO on the wall!). Keep right at a fork, then *left uphill* at the next fork (where a stronger path goes straight ahead). You join a fire-fighting road, which quickly becomes a track. Before the track makes a U-bend, be sure to *turn back sharp left* uphill on the waymarked route — a centuries-old trail. Climbing in zigzags, you enjoy fine views over Puget-Théniers and can trace the Var Valley from Utelle in the east to the castle at Entrevaux in the west. Reaching a CREST, walk (*carefully*) along the very top of the *robines* pouring down into the **Ravin du Planet** on your right.

Before long, the path moves away from the edge and heads west, leaving a little ruined house up above to the right. From a PASS (**1h**) you look ahead into the Roudoule Valley, backed by the Crête d'Aurafort (setting for the Alternative walk). As the walk continues uphill in tight zigzags, be sure to locate your waymarks. The **Roche d'Abeille** (**1h15min**) marks the top of the climb: from here there is a magnificent view east along the Var. The 'Bee's Rock' is a natural fortress, from where *robines* pour down into the Ravin du Planet. Walk on to ⌐173 and, at the fork, keep straight ahead, to the ruined **Bergerie de Lava** (**1h20min**), where you can take a break on the grassy slopes.

The onward walk starts from the back of the bergerie and descends to the Roudoule Valley, with views to the Crête d'Aurafort, the Castagnet Cliffs and the roofs of Puget-Théniers. This narrow path is especially beautiful in autumn, when wine-red Venetian sumac and gold grass contrast with the dark shiny leaves of the holm oaks. Here again, *care is needed* on the *robines*. Finally the path crosses a very narrow ridge between two *robines* — this only lasts for 12m/ yds, but is potentially dangerous on a windy day — and amazingly, this is when you return to

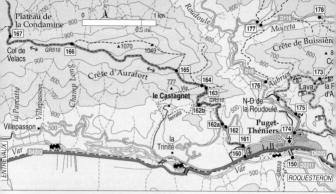

'civilisation' and are just above a house!

Join the drive to the house and, where it curves to the right, turn sharp left on a cart track. When this track turns towards a house, continue down a rough, grassy trail, making for the cemetery and telephone exchange. As you approach a wooden gate, turn sharp right down a footpath. Cross a gulley on a WOODEN FOOTBRIDGE and come to the **Rue de la Roudoule** (⚑175; **1h50min**). Turn left, follow the road down to ⚑174, and head back to **Puget-Théniers** and the STATION (**2h**).

View west across the Roudoule Valley to the Alternative walk — the Crête d'Aurafort and the Castagnet Cliffs above Puget-Théniers

Walk 26: GRES D'ANNOT

Distance: 5km/3mi; 2h15min
Grade: moderate climb/
descent of 330m/1100ft, but
you must be sure-footed on the
robines (see page 173 and Walk
25). Avoid the walk in mist or
wet weather. Yellow PR waymarking. *IGN map 3541 OT*
Equipment: see page 72;
walking stick(s). Refreshments
available at Annot
Travel: 🚌 to the railway
station at Annot (Car tour 6),
or 🚂 to Annot (Train des
Pignes; see page 168;
www.trainprovence.com)
**Short walk/picnic
suggestion: Notre-Dame-de-
Vers-la-Ville.** 25min return.
From the main square at
Annot, take the street at the
right of the fountain (a building arches over this street, and

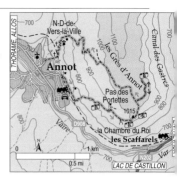

there is an *alimentation* on the
left and a *bar/tabac/hôtel* on the
right. Curve right into
Chemin de Vers-la-Ville; this
becomes a lane between fields
and then zigzags up past the 14
Stations of the Cross to the
chapel of **Notre-Dame**.

T his magnificent walk, beautifully shaded by oaks
and chestnuts, takes us through a chaos of
towering, eroded sandstone boulders, the Grès
d'Annot. Midway through the hike we skirt a cliff-face
below massive rock 'totem-poles', high above the confluence of the Vaïre and Coulomp at Les Scaffarels.

Start out at the RAILWAY
STATION at **Annot**: head downhill towards the village, then
turn right and walk through a
TUNNEL under the railway
(🟥: *CIRCUIT DES GRES D'ANNOT,
CHAMBRE DU ROI*). Out of the
tunnel, turn right on a stony
track, passing the octagonal
water tower for the old steam
trains. Keep along to the last
railway building (noticing the
house up to the left, built into
the first of the *grès* en route),
where the tracks disappear into
a shed (🟥: *ANNOT: ESCALADE
SUR LES GRES*). Just past the
sign, meet a fork and go left,
climbing slightly. When you
are directly above the turntable
for the old steam locomotives,

be sure to turn left in the first
zigzag of this stone-laid trail
(**10min**). Climb into the rock
chaos, where climbers have
inscribed mythological names
on the sandstone boulders.
Paths thread out in all directions; *keep careful watch for the
yellow waymarks.* If in doubt,
whenever possible follow paths
running parallel with the Vaïre
Valley on the right (climbing
southeast); don't head too far
left. Beyond the chaos you
should find yourself on the
stone-laid trail again (**30min**),
soon crossing some clay slopes
shored up with logs (*robines;*
see page 173 and Walk 25).
Five minutes later more
shored-up *robines* are crossed

137

At the Chambre du Roi

and there is a fine view to terracing on the far side of the Vaïre.

At a crossing of paths (**50min**), climb up to the right (❧: CHAMBRE DU ROI). In the shade of beautiful chestnuts you reach the narrow defile shown above. As you start into it, look right: ENTREE is written in red on a stone. If you're slim enough, and not claustrophobic, squat down and crawl through this opening, into the three huge rock 'rooms', illuminated by a small gap high above. Then return and continue through the towering, shady defile. At the end of the passage you come to a CLEARING with a fireplace and boulder-benches — a lovely picnic spot.

The path continues up to the cliff-edge above the confluence of roads and streams at Les Scaffarels, from where a fabulous 'balcony' path (amply wide, but watch your footing and *take special care* on windy days) carries you east in the setting shown opposite (**1h05min**), with beautiful views of innumerable cliffs and the Galange Gorge.

Once round the bluff, there are more breathtaking views over the apron of emerald cultivation skirting the Var. You now head inland through once-cultivated chestnut groves, which are losing ground to the faster-growing pines.

Detour: Soon a signposted path on the right indicates a possible detour north-northeast to a magnificent viewpoint over the Coulomp Valley and to the mountains beyond it. It's 15 minutes up and 10 minutes

138

These 'totem-pole' grès, 350m/1150ft above Les Scaffarels, mark the halfway point in the walk. The sandstone rocks in this area were once troglodyte dwellings and the stone was later used to face buildings in the old part of Annot.

back down; *not* included in our times. At first the route is well waymarked, but then the marks peter out, so you have to search out the best viewpoint in the far southeast corner; *take care; the drops are sheer!*) The main path climbs gently over bedrock and then through a mossy glen, full of ferns and tall trees embraced by ivy. You pass to the right of a ruined STONE SHELTER (**1h20min**) built below an overhang of rock, with a venerable chestnut in front. Now the path climbs quickly to the **Pas des Portettes**, the highest point of the walk. Turn left downhill here, passing under a high rock arch. (After you pass through it, turn round, since it is even more impressive from the far side.) Descending, follow the path round a bend to the right. As you come into another rock chaos, enjoy the lovely play of light and shade, as the sun streams through the magnificent chestnuts onto the moss-covered boulders. Once in a while, the path climbs *very slightly* before descending again, but *be sure not to climb too far up to the right.* Some seven-eight minutes below the pass, watch for your turn-off: you must go *sharp left* downhill. (If you find yourself walking north above Annot, you've gone too far.) Further downhill, several springs gush out over the path. which can be very wet at times, but it's pleasant to walk accompanied by the sound of running water.

You pass a building on the left dated 1672 and two minutes later come to the 12th-century chapel of **Notre-Dame-de-Vers-la-Ville** on the left (**1h55min**). Its wall-belfry is surmounted by a stone cross. From here a grassy stone-laid trail takes you downhill in zigzags, past the **14 Stations of the Cross**, each embellished with a naïve painting on glazed tiles. Cross the RAILWAY and follow a lane between colourful gardens and fields. When you come into **Annot**, head left on the main road. Turn left for GARE to get back to the STATION (**2h15min**).

139

Walk 27: AIGLUN AND THE ESTERON RIVER

Distance: 7.5km/4.7mi; 2h50min

Grade: moderate descent/ascent of 170m/560ft, but you must be sure-footed and agile for the initial descent. Yellow PR, red and white GR waymarking. *IGN map 3542 ET*

Equipment: see page 72; walking stick(s). Refreshments available at Aiglun

Travel: 🚗 (Car tour 7) to Aiglun. No 🚌 service at time of writing, but check www.departement06.fr/ vous-deplacer-en-bus/lignes-et-horaires-3029.html

Note: There used to be a path hugging the south side of the Esteron from the Pont de Végay to a suspension bridge below Vascognes (between signposts 85 and 86). At press date this path is closed because of a landslip, but the suspension bridge is still open. It's great fun, so after crossing the Pont de Végay, before you reach Vascognes, *do* turn right from ▮86a (see map) and have a look at the bridge — a good photo opportunity! It's unlikely that the path south of the river will ever reopen; we've deleted it from our map.

Alternative walk: Mont St-Martin. 10km/6.2mi; 5h. Strenuous, with an ascent/descent of about 800m/2130ft. Recommended for experienced, sure-footed walkers who find the main walk too 'tame'. Referring to the map, climb eastwards from Aiglun, with a beautiful view of the mountains in the south and east and down into the Esteron Valley. The yellow-waymarked path, signposted to Sallagriffon, then climbs north in steep zigzags. After about 30 minutes the terrain changes from woods to scree, with some ancient wind-sculpted oaks. From the Brèche du Mont St-Martin (▮76a) take the steep path to the summit, with a fine view north and northeast towards Sigale. Back at ▮76a, descend north past ▮76; about 15 minutes from the Brèche you come to ▮75c. Head left (southwest) here on a very narrow but good path for about half an hour, until you are above the Mont St-Martin climbing wall, where the path ends. You have a fantastic view into the walls of the Cluc d'Aiglun. Return the same way.

View back to Aiglun and the Clue d'Aiglun from the Esteron Valley

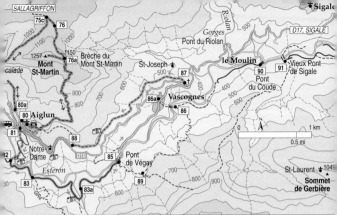

This circuit through pleasant oak woods in the Esteron Valley offers some fine views to the perched villages of Aiglun and Sigale — as well as a textbook introduction to Mediterranean fungi! But the bounding Esteron will be, without doubt, the focus of your attention. Those with plenty of energy will want to return to Aiglun to tackle the Alternative walk — with its fantastic view down into the Clue d'Aiglun. Another option, of course, is to just walk northwest along the D10 to signpost 80a, then take the path to where you can watch the climbers 'hanging' from the climbing wall ('Site d'escalade' on the map).

Start out in **Aiglun** at the MAIRIE: from ⌐81 descend paved steps and then a narrow, very stony path marked with yellow flashes. Below, you can see a bridge over the Esteron. Your path goes *straight* down to it, crossing an old lane and then a track. It's very steep; sometimes you'll be scrambling on all fours. When you drop down to this lovely old STONE BRIDGE (**25min**), cross it and, on the far side, turn left on a track. In a minute you pass ⌐82, where you join the GR4 and cross a tributary a minute later. Now look back to Aiglun, strung out between the walls of its *clue* and the cemetery chapel of Notre-Dame. In autumn, colonies of utterly revolting, slimy black fungi sprout along this track; our French textbook assures us

that they are *coprin à chevelure* and edible!
At ⌐83 (**35min**) continue ahead for PONT DE VEGAY. About eight minutes later there is a view south to the Cascade de Végay (not on our map) from a signpost indicating a path up to the falls. Ignore the sign; continue ahead past a lovely rock pool. Around here the diagonal strata in the orange cliffs draw your attention — as does Sigale, straddling the cliffs up ahead, beyond the Riolan Gorge.
At the **Pont de Végay** (⌐85; **1h05min**, turn left and cross the bridge. Turn right on the little lane on the far side and follow it for a little over 1km, to **Vascognes** (**1h25min**). Continue on the lane to the D10 (**1h40min**) and turn left. Pass a SHRINE on the right and,

141

View towards Sigale from Vascognes, with the Esteron River below

just beyond it, turn right up a concrete lane (▪87). Quickly coming to wrought-iron gates, you meet a fork: go left just *before* the gates, following a footpath. At a Y-fork almost immediately, go right on a grassy path. All the climbing to regain height is done on this pretty, shady path, through oaks and broom. It is narrow but very well waymarked; follow the waymarks *carefully*, so as not to miss any U-turns.

Passing under the rock needles of the **Bau du Bouquet**, the climb levels out (**2h10min**), and there are more views back down the valley to Sigale. It's a pity to leave the birdsong of this bower, but soon the path deposits you on the D10 again, at ▪88 (**2h35min**). Turn right and follow the road for 1km, back to **Aiglun** (**2h50min**). There's another fine view to the Végay falls as you pass below Notre-Dame.

Right: the Lac de Castillon (Walk 28 and Car tours 5 and 7). During Car tour 5 you skirt the full length of this huge man-made lake, a mirror of sparkling reflections. Notice the folds of beige earth streaming down the slopes; these are robines, *outpourings of crumbly, limey-clay soil. They are prevalent throughout Alpes de Haute-Provence; we call them 'elephants', and you'll soon realise why! Walks 25 and 26 cross many robines.*

Walk 28: VILLE

Distance: 2.5km/1.5mi; 1h
Grade: easy (ascent: 60m/
165ft). No waymarking. *IGN
map 3542 OT*
Equipment: stout shoes;
refreshments available in
Demandolx
Travel: 🚗 to the U-bend of
the C2 2km west of Deman-
dolx (Car tour 7). Park at the
side of the track (with a metal
barrier). No 🚌 service

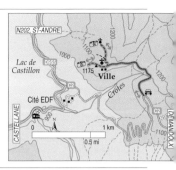

This stroll to the ruined hamlet of Ville, and the short hike up to the chapel beyond it, afford incredibly beautiful views over the turquoise Lac de Castillon, edged by beige *robines* and lush green alpine slopes.

Start out on the C2: follow the track, below beautifully-striated cliffs, to the ruins of **Ville** (**15min**). Just past the end of the track, *before* the first house of the hamlet (with an orange paint blob), the path on the right will be your ongoing route. After exploring the ruins, walk out to the grassy promontory beyond them for breathtaking views of the lake and dam.
Then go back to the path passed earlier and turn left uphill. Ignore two clear forks to the left as you rise in

zigzags. Beyond a tall stone CAIRN/SHRINE, turn left and walk through globe thistles, box and pines — to a CHAPEL on a grassy knoll (**40min**). You should see two tall Disney-like structures on the hill opposite — at Blaron, home of the Aumist religious sect. We still call them the 'Three Kings', although the central, 100ft-high statue of their leader was blown up in 2001 by Castellane Council for blighting the landscape.
From here retrace your steps to the C2 (**1h**).

Walk 29: CIRCUIT AROUND COMPS-SUR-ARTUBY

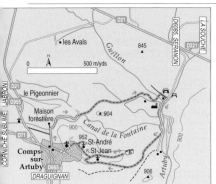

Equipment: see page 72; stout shoes will suffice. Refreshments available at Comps

Travel: 🚌 to Comps (Car tour 7), then drive east on the D21 towards *DIGNE* (green sign). But 2km along, just before the D221 goes left to La Souche, turn right to a picnic area by a factory. No 🚐 service

Hint: At the junction of the D21 and D221, go left on the D221; just past La Souche there is a lovely Roman bridge over the Artuby — one of many splendid picnic spots in this area.

Distance: 3km/2mi; 1h10min
Grade: easy ascent/descent of about 100m/330ft. Green and white, some blue and yellow PR waymarking. *IGN map 3543 OT*

T his very short walk, an ideal leg-stretcher, visits a delightful chapel and the 13th-century church of St-André, from where you can survey the beautiful green fields around Comps and look out to the mountains edging the Gorges du Verdon.

Start out at the PICNIC AREA: walk south along the lane, with the FACTORY on the right and a RIVER POOL on the left. Just 1m/yd *before* two PILLARS on the lane, climb the green/white-waymarked path on the right. This grassy path, sometimes shaded by pines, rises between bluffs, above the **Artuby River**. Some 400m/yds uphill, just *past* a white 'change of direction' waymark, be sure to turn uphill to the right at a huge CAIRN (where another path runs straight ahead).

Soon the path levels out, and Comps is visible ahead. To the left, on the far side of the Artuby Gorge, is the little Notre-Dame chapel that makes such a lovely picnic spot on Car tour 7. When a cart track comes in from the left behind you, join it and continue ahead. Before the track becomes tarred, turn right up

steps, to the **Chapelle St-Jean** (**25min**). Now follow the crest behind the chapel, take in the views (including Robion in the north and the twin ruined towers of Bargème in the near northeast), before walking on to the 13th-century church/chapel of **St-André** (**35min**), with its beautifully-made water tank.

From here take the walkway down through Comps, to the D955. Then turn right on the lane adjacent to the MAIRIE/POSTE (the *boulangerie* will be on your left). Ignore a track off to the left 100m/yds along. 60m/yds further on, turn right downhill (YELLOW/BLUE WAYMARKS on a pylon), into another mini-gorge. The way becomes a path and emerges in a grassy area at the left-hand edge of conifers. Do *not* head down left into the valley here; keep contouring, so that you soon have conifers on both sides. Watch for an open-sided storage shed ahead, below you; your path runs to the left of it, *just to the left of the factory fence* (which soon becomes visible). Once you pass the barn, the path descends a bit more steeply *and crosses a ditch*. Turn right on a track on the far side of the ditch, back to the PICNIC AREA (**1h10min**).

Comps-sur-Artuby, with the St-Jean chapel (right) and the 13th-century Gothic church of St-André (left).

Walk 30: ABOVE TOURTOUR

Distance: 7.5km/4.7mi; 1h55min

Grade: easy, with ascents/descents of 120m/400ft overall; little shade. No consistent waymarking, but easily followed. *IGN map 3443 OT*

Equipment: see page 72; stout shoes will suffice. Refreshments available at Tourtour

Travel: 🚗 to Tourtour (Car tour 7). No 🚌 service

Short walk: Moulières. 3.5km/2.2mi; 55min. Easy; access by 🚗. There is a large parking area beside FIRE TRACK K45 at **Moulières** (see map). Start and end the walk there, perhaps visiting the Tour de Grimaldi as well.

Alternative walk: Tour de Grimaldi. 9km/5.6mi; 2h20min. From the 17min-point in the main walk, make a detour to the Tour de Grimaldi (on a lane).

The hamlets of Moulières — old and new — are the focal points of this walk, but you will also enjoy fine views back to Tourtour and ahead to the Maures and Esterel, as you cross a textbook example of *garrigues*. The walk is best done in spring, when the limestone-loving vegetation is in full flower.

Start out at the multi-spouted FOUNTAIN in the main square in **Tourtour**: facing the traffic lights and signs to Aups and Salernes, walk half-right for 80m/yds, to a T-junction. This is **Rue du Lavoir**: turn left. You climb north past a fort on the left and the old — but still used — washing place (*lavoir*) on the right. Further to the right are verdant fields. Fork left in front of a large IRON CROSS and a tiny CHAPEL (**6min**). At a junction six minutes later, go straight across the D51. Ignore the lane off left to the Grimaldi Tower

(**17min**). (*The Alternative walk heads left here, for a short detour to the Tour Grimaldi.*)
Beyond a handful of elegant properties, you cross a STREAM (**25min**) in the latter-day hamlet of **Moulières**, where the rustic houses, poplar woods, and splendid vegetable and flower gardens are a delight.
Pass FIRE TRACK K45 off to the right (your return route and parking for the Short walk). Almost immediately, at the junction (**30min**), curve right on the lane. You pass a drive off left to a house and the lane peters out into a track. Some 40 paces futher on, turn right on FIRE TRACK K66, through a stand of cypresses. Ignore a track off to the right after 30 paces. Now climb above the valley on a stony track. Seven minutes along, go straight over

Tourtour's church (right), and the village from the Rue du Lavoir (below)

Poplar wood near fire track K45 at Moulières (above), and the old mill beside the watercourse (left)

a crossing track, to pass to the left of the summit of **Camp Redon**. Aups is visible in the distance now, to the right of a quarry.

When the track that passed to the east of Redon comes in from behind and to the right, continue left downhill under the welcome shade of pines. Below a rocky crag up on your left, you come to a fork. Turn right on *FIRE TRACK K45* (K66 continues ahead) and, at the next fork, go right again. You cross the **Aigue Blanche** stream bed (**55min**) and come to a T-junction. Turn right here. Two minutes later, ignore a track off to the left; keep ahead on a narrower trail, straight towards the poplars at Moulières. Six minutes after

that, ignore another track off left (although it has yellow flash waymarks). But four minutes later, at a Y-fork, *do turn left:* curl steeply downhill to another track, passing huge ancient oaks on the right. You've entered a grotto just behind the poplar wood, and a watercourse (which you may find sadly dry) is on your right. At another fork, a couple of minutes along, again go left — to the ruins of the old hamlet and mill of **Moulières** (**1h15min**). Pause a while in this lovely ferny glen, where light and shade play over the ruins and contorted rocks beside the stream. (Since this is a very short walk, you may like to continue for a while beside the watercourse on the gorgeous grassy path in this mini-gorge, the **Vallon des Moulières**.)

Then return the same way, but keep left at the first fork, to follow *FIRE TRACK K45* back to **Moulières** (**1h20min**). Then turn left and retrace your steps to **Tourtour** (**1h55min**).

Walk 31: SENTIER MARTEL

See also photos pages 52-55
Distance: 14km/8.7mi; 6h
Grade: moderate-strenuous, with 450m/1475ft of descent and 350m/1150ft of ascent overall. Two tunnels en route, one of them 700m/0.4mi long. The initial descent is steep, and there is a further descent at the Brèche Imbert, down a metal 'staircase' (250 steps; see photograph overleaf), where you must be sure-footed and have a head for heights. Red and white GR waymarking. While the walk *can* be done in either direction, it is best started from the La Maline end — there is less of a climb at the end (*if* you leave your car at the Samson Corridor), less heat reflecting from the gorge walls, and better conditions for photography. *IGN map 3442 OT*
Note: Remember that the Verdon supplies a battery of factories and hydroelectric stations; it is dangerous to venture too far off the riverbank; the water can rise very suddenly without warning.
Equipment: see page 72; *torch, plenty of water,* warm clothing. Refreshments available at La Maline and Point Sublime
Travel: 🚗 to Point Sublime (Car tour 8); *leave nothing of value in your car.*
Here you will find taxis (or can telephone for a taxi). The taxi driver will ask you to move your car to the Samson Corridor, from where he will take you 18km west to the Chalet de la Maline, where the walk starts. In summer *only*, a shuttle 🚐 runs from Castellane to Point Sublime and then La Maline, a much cheaper option (usually leaves Point Sublime at 08.45, arriving La Maline at 09.20; timetables at www.lapaludsurverdon.com/images/transports/Navette_Sentier_Martel.pdf or 📞 04 92 34 22 90). If you take this bus, from the end of the walk at the Samson Corridor, it's an additional climb of 150m/500ft back to your car at Point Sublime via the GR4.

Short walk: Baume aux Pigeons. 3km/2mi; 1h. Easy, but you need a *torch*). Park at the **Samson Corridor**: the road (D236) is under 1km east of the inn at Point Sublime (Car tour 8). From the PARKING BAY at the end of this road, follow the GR4 (red and white waymarks) as far as the steps in the tunnel, descend (if you like) to the river, and return the same way. *Very crowded on weekends and in the summer.*
Alternative walk: Brèche Imbert. 12km/7.5mi; 5h30min. Moderate; access/equipment as for the Short walk. Follow the GR4 as far as the metal staircase at the Brèche Imbert; return the same way.

T his is *the* classic itinerary in Provence, and arguably the most beautiful (and crowded) walk in all Europe. At the height of the season, more than 2500 people *a day* pass through the Samson Corridor (after 80 years the walk was totally repaired between 2011-2013). *Do* try to go in spring or autumn, mid-week, to make the most of this unforgettable experience.

The dramatic descent at the Brèche Imbert, down some 250 steps

Start out facing the **Chalet de la Maline**: take the GR4 footpath at the northeast side of the building. After rounding a ravine, the path descends from the **Pas d'Issane** in hairpins *(keep to the zigzags, to prevent further erosion)*. Dropping to a junction, turn

left on the **Sentier Martel**
(**50min**). E-A Martel (see Car
tour 8, page 50, was the first
person to explore the depths of
the gorge, in 1905 —
commissioned by the company
who planned to built a 25km-
long watercourse from
Carejuan to Galetas. The
project was abandoned during
World War I, but is the reason
for all the tunnels and screes
along the route. A few more
zigzags take you to a 'balcony'
path 10m/30ft above the river.

Look up across the canyon to
the Auberge des Cavaliers atop
the cliff. Now follow the right
bank of the river upstream.
You might miss the **Pré
d'Issane**, some 30 minutes
along, but there is evidence
that man cultivated this river
bank meadow even in
prehistoric times.
The path then rises to the
Guègues scree, which is
crossed via metal stairs with a
handrail. A little over 10
minutes beyond here, watch

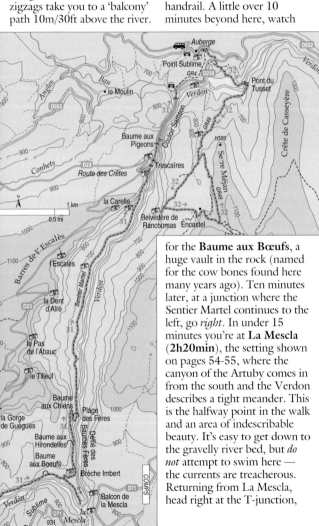

for the **Baume aux Bœufs**,
a huge vault in the rock (named
for the cow bones found here
many years ago). Ten minutes
later, at a junction where the
Sentier Martel continues to the
left, go *right*. In under 15
minutes you're at **La Mescla**
(**2h20min**), the setting shown
on pages 54-55, where the
canyon of the Artuby comes in
from the south and the Verdon
describes a tight meander. This
is the halfway point in the walk
and an area of indescribable
beauty. It's easy to get down to
the gravelly river bed, but *do
not* attempt to swim here —
the currents are treacherous.
Returning from La Mescla,
head right at the T-junction,

The first tunnel is bypassed, as you enter the Sampson Corridor

climbing steeply to the **Brèche Imbert** (**3h**), named for the engineer who opened this crevice for walkers. As you look straight down 120m/400ft to the river below, *descend the metal staircase slowly and carefully*. Once back down on *terra firma*, you climb below the **Baume aux Hirondelles** and then descend in a U-turn, to pass below the **Baume aux Chiens**. After meeting the river at the **Plage des Fères**, you climb again below the steep orange cliffs of the **Escalès**, rising 500m/1650ft above you (photograph page 52). You may spot climbers on the really sheer part of these cliffs, further east.

After passing to the right of a first TUNNEL (disused and dangerous), you enter the **Samson Corridor**. Beyond a short flight of metal stairs, 152

there is a fine view back to the twin rock turrets of **Les Trescaïres** (see page 52). Go through the next two TUNNELS, the second of which has 'windows' to brighten the gloom. At the first 'window', another flight of metal stairs lead down to the river, at the huge **Baume aux Pigeons**. Beyond this tunnel, turn back to look up at 'Samson' in his white robe (on the left bank), in his futile attempt to push apart the canyon walls. Now the path descends stone-cut steps to the river bed, crosses the **Bau Stream** on a foot-bridge, and comes to the parking area in the **Samson Corridor** (**6h**). Those who have left their cars at Point Sublime now face a final climb of 150m/500ft up the GR4 (from the far left-hand side of the car park).

Walk 32: BELVEDERE DE RANCOUMAS

See also photographs page 52

Distance: 8km/5mi; 3h30min

Grade: fairly strenuous ascents/descents of 600m/2000ft overall. Good, shady paths. Red and white GR, sparse yellow PR waymarking. One pathless section requires a good sense of direction. *IGN map 3442 OT*

Equipment: see page 72; warm clothing in cold weather. There is a spring (sometimes dry) at the 50min-point; refreshments available at Point Sublime

Travel: 🚌 to the car park at Point Sublime (Car tour 8). *Leave nothing of value in your car.* 🚐: see Walk 31, page 149.

Short walk: Pont du Tusset. 2km/1.2mi; under 1h. Easy descent/ascent of 200m/650ft; stout shoes will suffice. Follow the main walk for 25min and return the same way.

Two gorgeous, but little frequented beauty spots in the Verdon are the highlights of this walk — the old Roman bridge below Point Sublime and an emerald eyrie opposite the Escalès climbing edge, with plunging views into the gorge.

The Pont du Tusset. In autumn Venetian sumach (Cotinus coggygria), prized for flower arrangements, lights up all the slopes in Haute-Provence.

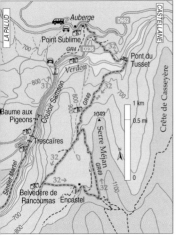

Start out at the inn at **Point Sublime**: walk downhill towards CAREJUAN. After 100m, just in front of an INFORMATION PANEL about the Sentier Martel (Walk 31), turn right down a footpath, following the red and white waymarks of the GR4 and GR49. At a fork in three minutes, go left with the GR49 (the GR4 goes right to the Samson Corridor). At a Y-fork almost immediately, bear right downhill. Cross the access road to the Samson Corridor and follow the stony track ahead (☞: SENTIER D'ENCASTEL). At a junction, ignore the path to the right (marked with a red and white 'X'); turn left down a narrow path through mixed oaks sprinkled with conifers (☞: GR49). Soon you hear the sound of rushing water. Three minutes past the junction, ignore a path to the left (also marked with an 'X').
After a descent of 200m/650ft, you're on the 2000-year-old **Pont du Tusset** (**25min**), crossing the roaring turquoise river. Just beyond the bridge,

curve uphill to the right *(part of the path may be broken away here; watch your step)*. Some Montpellier maples grace the path, together with the Venetian sumac shown on page 153. You pass a SPRING on your left (**50min**); if it's not dry, its gurgling will alert you to it. Further up, when you are level with the viewpoint at Point Sublime, there are fine views over to the village of Rougon. Some 15 minutes past the spring, begin climbing in zigzags. At a fork where the GR49 curls up to the left in a U-turn (**1h20min**; our return route); keep *right* on a good, but narrow path, where you may notice some faded yellow waymarks. (Don't confuse the forestry signs here with GR flashes; see notes on page 73.)
A stream is crossed about five minutes past the fork. Beyond the stream, bear left uphill at a Y-fork. The walk soon levels out, and you're on a high PLATEAU (**1h 30min**), deep in the golden grasses of abandoned terraces, now invaded by junipers and wild roses. Keep heading in the same direction, with the walls of the canyon on your right, and soon you will spot a patch of emerald green ahead. Just before you get there, notice the path joining you from the left; it is marked with cairns and faded yellow waymarks; this is your ongoing route.
The grassy **Belvédère de Rancoumas** (**1h40min**) is a sun-trap and a perfect picnic spot. The canyon walls fall 400m/1300ft below you here. Can you bear to look over the edge? Opposite, to the left, is the (100m/300ft higher) climbing wall of the **Escalès** on the

north bank (photograph page 52), with the Sentier Martel below it; to the right you can spot the railings at the Belvédère des Trescaïres; these twin turrets, shown on page 52, are below you to the right.

From the viewpoint head east along the path passed earlier, through a splurge of broom, lavender, heather and pines. Coming over a small rise, you see the old hamlet of **Encastel** ahead, surrounded by green pastures. Skip down to it and pass to the *right* of the house that is intact and to the left of the ruins, on a level grassy trail. *Now take care, as there are no waymarks.* When the trail reduces to a barely-perceptible path (and you have lost sight of the ruins because of foliage), *keep more or less on a level contour, while moving slightly to the left* (don't climb up right or *descend* to the left). You might encounter wild boar around here — we never have, but some correspondents report sightings. If you do see any wild boar, it is always a good idea to give them a wide berth.

Going through more abandoned terraces, you pass a WATERING HOLE, come into woodland, and meet a strong crossing path on a bend (**2h**). Follow this lovely woodland path (GR49) down to the fork first encountered at the 1h20min-point in the walk. Turn down right here, in the hairpin bend, and retrace your outgoing route. Take on water at the SPRING; it's a tiring climb back up to **Point Sublime** (**3h30min**).

As you look towards the north bank from the Belvédère de Rancoumas, the canyon walls are so close together that it's hard to believe there's a 400m drop to the river between them!

Walk 33: CHARTREUSE DE LA VERNE

Distance: 5km/3mi; 1h35min
Grade: easy ascent/descent of about 130m/425ft overall. Little shade. Blue, then yellow PR waymarking. *IGN map 3545 OT*
Equipment: see page 72;

refreshments at Collobrières, Grimaud
Travel: 🚌 to the Chartreuse de la Verne (Car tour 9). Open 11am-5pm (6pm in summer). Closed Tue (ex Jun-Aug), 25 Dec, Easter. No 🚐 service

Early October is a good time to visit the Chartreuse, if only to enjoy the antics of the local chestnut-gatherers. This walk gives a fine variety of views, especially over to the sea and the Gulf of St-Tropez.

Start out at the **Chartreuse de la Verne**. Walk past the south front (shown below right). At the fork that follows immediately, take the upper route to the right, rising through a beautiful sweet chestnut wood on a lane. Despite all the notices prohibiting the taking of chestnuts, in autumn the locals will be gathered en masse to collect them, with large tables for sorting — and, later, picnicking.

Pass a SPRING on the right (**7min**). Just as the lane makes a U-turn to the right, keep left on a track (faded BLUE FLASHES on rocks underfoot). Almost immediately you have a brilliant view over a reservoir and the Gulf of St-Tropez. The chestnuts have given way to holm oaks and *garrigues;* there are fine, open views. After crossing a second stream, you look north-northeast towards white crystalline rocks on the highest ridge in the Maures

(the Roches Blanches), with the mountains of Haute-Provence behind them, and northeast to Grimaud with its

Above right: The south front of the Chartreuse de la Verne. The buildings are well hidden in the green, green forests of the Maures. Right: early in the walk there's a lovely view down over a reservoir (Barrage de la Verne) and to the Gulf of St-Tropez in the distance.

156

twin towers, backed by the Rocher de Roquebrune and the Esterel.

At a junction of FIRE TRACKS (**35min**), you pass a turn-off left near the summit of **L'Argentière**. Ignore the 'Noyer' track to the left; keep ahead on SIVADIERES, passing the **Refuge des Sivadières** on the right, in a pretty grove of oaks. Strawberry trees and heather line this stretch, while vineyards edge the D98 below on the left.

At a Y-junction below the **Sommet du Péra** (**55min**),

turn sharp right on a tarred lane (⌐: *ROUTE DE LA CRETE*, now rounding the west side of **L'Ermitage**. The relay at Notre-Dame-des-Anges can be seen to the left, with the Montagne Sainte-Victoire behind it.

At the following junction there is a CISTERN on the left; walk ahead to a 'no entry' sign with a YELLOW FLASH and take the footpath behind it. This leads through more chestnut woods, back to the **Chartreuse de la Verne** (**1h35min**).

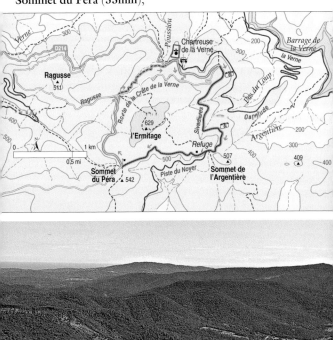

Walk 34: CAP LARDIER

Distance: 8km/5mi; 3h
Grade: fairly easy-moderate, with ascents/descents of 250m/820ft overall. Some agility is required. The walk is very exposed to sun *and wind*. Yellow PR waymarking. *IGN map 3545 OT*
Equipment: see page 72; swimming things, ample sun protection. Refreshments available at Gigaro
Travel: 🚌 to Gigaro (detour on Car tour 9). From the D93 between Ramatuelle and La Croix-Valmer, follow sign-posting for *GIGARO*. Once on the coast, drive along the esplanade and park where the road turns inland. No 🚐 service

Short walk: Les Pins Blancs. 5.5km/3.4mi; 2h05min. Fairly easy. Follow the main walk for 55min, then either return the same way or take the inland route by picking up the main walk from the 2h05min-point.

This coastal walk is really amazing. If you wish, and if you can arrange transport, you can follow the shore with very few interruptions all the way to the centre of St-Tropez. It's almost too good to be true that some 30km of pristine coastline has been saved from development and is currently a conservation area. You will pass gorgeous beaches, picnic amidst a bouquet of wild flowers, and enjoy refreshing sea breezes.

Start out in **Gigaro**, just where the road skirting the esplanade turns inland. Here you pick up the coastal footpath (▐: *SENTIER LITTORAL*). The information panel here shows various routes in the area and estimated walking times; our route is waymarked in yellow.

Follow the sandy path under the shade of false acacias. As soon as you leave the main part of Gigaro's beach, you will see very few people taking advantage of the isolated coves, each with its own tiny sandy beach, set apart from the others by fingers of rock. Yellow-flowering sneezewort (*Achillea*) grows all along the cliff here. Having crossed a creek, you come to a lovely group of umbrella pines, **Les Pins Parasols (15min)**. This is just one of many idyllic settings for a picnic.

Beyond the **Plage de Jovat (25min)** the way divides, and a green-waymarked footpath, the Sentier du Brouis, climbs inland. Keep right, along the beach. Five minutes later you pass a beach hut, the **Cabanon du Pêcheur**. Not long after, you reach the **Pointe du Brouis**. Beyond here the path is less 'tame', and there are few people about. Now you descend towards the beach through thistles and grasses — in early summer, this path is a medley of lavender- and gold-flowering plants.

Passing behind the **Plage du Brouis (45min)**, head right when you come to a fork (don't go left up into the umbrella pines). This takes you to a major, signposted junction, where Gigaro is back to the left. Go right here (▐: *CAP LARDIER*), ploughing through the sand, then quickly regaining the earthen path, which is so much easier underfoot. Now a steep climb (sometimes a scramble, where you will need to use your hands) takes you up to a PASS where there is a track and a few tall umbrella pines (**Les Pins Blancs; 55min**).

Turn right through a sea of purple thistles and gold grasses. In a minute you come to another signpost: to the left a path waymarked in green climbs a conical hill to a ruined forestry house (La Bastide Blanche). Our route is to the right (▐: *CAP LARDIER, CAP*

Parasol pines and cooling sea breezes add to the exhilaration of this coastal walk. Remember that the breeze can be deceptively cooling; always take sun protection!

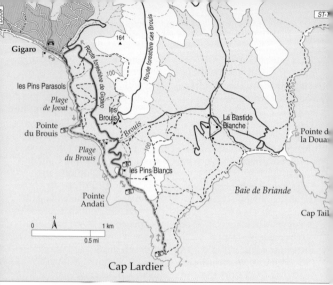

Gigaro's parasol pines

and St-Tropez. But climb back the way you came and, just beyond the signpost for Cap Lardier (at Les Pins Blancs; **2h05min**), fork right (↑: *GIGARO PAR L'INTERIEUR*). Almost immediately, fork right again (↑: *PISTE FORESTIERE PRINCIPALE*). Soon this wide track curves round to give lovely views over the sea again, and down to the coastal path. Over on the right is one of the most beautiful forests of umbrella pines you'll ever see — the hillside is a pin-cushion of emerald-green velvet, padded with the gentle mounds of these luminous, soft-needled trees.

Twenty minutes along the track, you could head back to the sea for a swim, when you pass a left turn down to the Plage du Brouis. Or continue on the sun-baked track, through cork oaks and large quaking grass (*Briza maxima*, easily recognised by its shrimp-shaped head). Beyond the information panels, return to your car at **Gigaro** (**3h**).

TAILLAT). Head right, under kermes oaks. The path levels out as you look down on a gorgeous turquoise sea. Butterflies abound here, as does white-flowering Montpellier cistus and the red-berried mastic bush *(Pistacia lentiscus)*. The route descends gently, joining a track coming in from the left.

From the old BATTERY at **Cap Lardier** (**1h30min**) the path continues east to Cap Taillat

160

Walk 35: LA MONTAGNE STE-VICTOIRE

See also photographs pages 4-5, 70

Distance: 11km/6.8mi; 4h
Grade: strenuous; ascent/descent of 600m/1970ft. The trails and paths are *very stony* underfoot. *The descent over loose stones takes almost as long as the climb.* **Allow plenty of time (at least 6h) for this walk, especially in hot weather.** Set off as early as possible and hope for a cool, *but not windy* day. Red and white GR waymarking. *IGN map 3244 ET; see also map recommended on page 7.*
NB: Some paths on the Ste-Victoire massif may be closed to walkers between 21 June and 30 September, if the risk of forest fires is high. Check at www.paca.gouv.fr/files.massif (map updated daily).
Equipment: see page 72; walking stick(s), warm clothing in cold weather. Allow **two litres of water per person** (there are no springs en route, and the well at the summit doesn't always work). Refreshments available at Vauvenargues (2km)
Travel: 🚌 to Les Cabassols, 2km west of Vauvenargues on the D10 (Car tour 10); park at the parking area by the bus shelter. Or 🚌 to Les Cabassols (Vauvenargues bus from Aix; www.agglo-paysdaix.fr/transports)

Ｏne of the most famous hikes in the South of France, the ascent of Ste-Victoire is a 'must'. We have taken the classic route, which follows the GR9 up the north side of the mountain. *Technically* the walk is easy. But this is a brutal mountain— sun-baked, wind-blasted, stony and hostile. Choose your day carefully! Ideally you want to be walking on a clear but still, cool day between October and early May.

Start out at the BUS SHELTER at **Les Cabassols**. Follow a path heading left (east) out of the parking area (☞: PRIEURE DE STE-VICTOIRE). The path, with red and white GR waymarks, takes you *downhill* — disheartening, since you know it will only add to the total ascent! At a fork met immediately, bear right. At the next fork, again go right, down a stony path. You cross a STREAM (**5min**). Just beyond it, at another fork, again go right downhill. Then fork right for a fourth time, rounding a METAL GATE. The hamlet of Les Cabassols is left behind, and you finally begin the ascent (**10min**). At any fork watch for GR waymarks —

particularly 15 minutes uphill, where paths go either side of a kermes oak grove: keep right. The first notable LANDMARK on this tedious uphill slog comes up when the trail forks round either side of pine trees twice in succession (**55min**). (Climbing in hot weather, we reached this point in 1h10min *including stops,* and it took us 2h30min to get to the chapel, so these trees are a good indication of how long it will

take *you* to get to the top.) After about an hour, you may be amazed at how much ground you've covered; while the chapel is still a long way off, at least it now seems within reach. The Pic des Mouches, the highest summit on Ste-Victoire (1011m/ 3316ft) is seen rising on the far left.

The stony trail ends at spot height 722m, where there is a METAL SEAT (**1h25min**). Take a break here, before continuing straight uphill on a narrow footpath. By the time the path begins to climb in zigzags, you

Left: the Prieuré Notre-Dame, with the Croix de Provence behind it. The Brèche des Moines is the cutting to the right, below the cross. Below: Ste-Victoire from the D17, with the Croix de Provence clearly visible. The paths that ascend the mountain from this south side are much more demanding than the GR9.

will be above the tree-line, crossing *garrigues*. The sun can be brutal now, but at least the deep hairpin bends take the strain off the lungs. Do watch for the waymarks here, being sure to turn sharply into the zigzags. (There are many short-cuts off these hairpin bends; *please don't use them:* they cost too much energy *and* they erode the main path.) Eventually the lovely valley at Vauvenargues is seen below (**1h45min**), and there is a fine view west over the tail of the turquoise-blue Bimont Reservoir. As you near the summit, in a shower of wild flowers, notice that the limestone mule trail is worn to a white-marble shine by centuries of footfalls. Just beyond another metal bench surrounded by irises and daisies, you reach the 17th-century chapel shown opposite, the **Prieuré Notre-Dame** (**2h10min**). It is set in a limestone cradle, with a cross rising on a rocky spit 60m/ 200ft above it. Nearby is a simple refuge, completely bare except perhaps for a pile of wood. There is also a well here, but it's not always in working order.

From the refuge walk towards the rock cutting on the south side of the mountain, *taking care to avoid the huge pit behind the pine tree.* As soon as you reach this colossal **Brèche des Moines** (Monks' Gap), you will probably sink to your knees like everyone else, as the abyss below you is revealed. Now you will see why we chose the northern ascent; the paths coming up from the south are difficult and vertiginous.

No doubt you will want to

continue up to the cross — the beacon that rises over all the walks and tours around the mountain. The scramble up to it requires agility and, while it's not difficult, the boot-polished rocks are very slippery. However, coming back down, it is easy to miss the main path, in which case you could find yourself on a very awkward and vertiginous scree slope. So *pay close attention to the path you take up to the cross*.

Clamber up to the **Croix de Provence** (**2h20min**). It's certainly worth the effort, because there is a tiny METAL HUT cum viewing platform up here. Those of us who suffer from vertigo can stand in the protection of its walls and look straight down the south side of the mountain, where the bright limestone cliffs are embedded in vivid red clay. Here the Ste-Baume massif rises beyond the valley of the Arc to the southeast. The Barrage de Bimont glimmers in the

northwest, where the Lubéron drops down to the Durance. In the east, beyond the Pic des Mouches, the Provençal Alps seem a hazy mirage. Dedicated on 18 May 1875 (and restored in 1983), the massive cross is strung with lights. It's hard to imagine how anyone could have put them there or, indeed, how such a huge structure was raised in this vertiginous spot, some 30m/100ft above the mountain spine.

Having returned to the chapel (sometimes on all fours), descend overlooking the Bimont Reservoir and the Cause Valley. Unfortunately, this descent on *very* loose stones is even more tiring than the ascent. Back at the SEAT at spot height 722m (**3h**), the path becomes a trail. At the fork by the kermes oak grove (first passed 15 minutes uphill) be sure to go left. After crossing the stream, you rise back to **Les Cabassols** (**4h**).

If you stay in the area and do Walk 36, after an easy stroll to the Zola dam you'll be able to look up to the summit of Ste-Victoire and say 'I was there!'.

Walk 36: LAC ZOLA

See also photographs pages 69 and opposite
Distance: 6.5km/4mi; 2h10min
Grade: fairly easy, with ascents/descents of 250m/820ft overall. Good, if rather stony, tracks and paths under foot. Varied waymarking colours. *IGN map 3244 ET; see also map recommended on page 7.*
NB: Some paths on the Ste-Victoire massif may be closed to walkers between 21 June and 30 September, if the risk of forest fires is high. Check at www.paca.gouv.fr/files.massif (map updated daily).
Equipment: see page 72; swimming things. Refreshments available at Aix-en-Provence (6km)
Travel: 🚌 to Le Tholonet (park in the parking area opposite the château; Car tour 10), or 🚌 from Aix to Le Tholonet (www.agglo-paysdaix.fr/transports
Alternative walks
1 Aqueduc de Doudon.
8km/5mi; 2h45min. Ascents/descents of 300m/1000ft overall. Follow the main walk for 1h, then continue ahead along the track, to the AQUEDUCT that carries water from the Bimont Reservoir to the plains south of Aix. Turn left here and, at a crossing track with GREEN WAYMARKS, turn left again. Rejoining the main walk south of **Lac Zola**, follow it to the end.
2 Lac de Bimont. 12.5km/7.8mi; 4h. Ascents/descents of 350m/1150ft overall. Do Alternative walk 1 above but, when you meet the track waymarked in green, keep right. Continue on a track with RED WAYMARKS, to the DAM at the **Lac de Bimont**. Return the same way, then turn right on the track with GREEN WAYMARKS, to get to **Lac Zola**. Rejoin the main walk at the 1h25min-point. *Or: cross* the **Bimont** DAM and take the GR653A path with YELLOW/

This delightful hike takes you to a very pretty small lake, with pleasant views to the cross atop Ste-Victoire. On the way we make a detour into a shady grotto and then pass the remains of a Roman aqueduct.

Start out at the CHATEAU in **Le Tholonet**. Walk west along the D17 for 250m/yds, then turn right on the **Chemin de la Paroisse** (WALKERS' FINGER-POST AND MAP). When you come to a knoll on the right, turn right on the wide path marked by WALKERS' INFORMATION BOARDS AND MAPS, at first rising parallel with the lane. The path widens out, and you head east through pines and holm oak to the base of a rocky outcrop. After passing above the BACK OF THE CHATEAU (**15min**), the path curves to the left and drops. At a fork go either way — just head for the sound of rushing water below. After a short steep descent, you come to a narrow IRRIGATION DITCH: turn left on the path beside it (it's slightly overgrown at first, but then excellent). You come to a FORD SHADED BY PLANE TREES (**25min**), an unusual setting for a picnic. (If you are intrigued by offbeat places, continue ahead a short way past the ford, to where the stream threads through gorges, and some intrepid explorers

This plane-tree shaded ford near the start of the walk is a lovely place for a picnic on a hot day, before you start the flower-filled descent to Lac Zola.

have made a 'path' through the wilderness with logs and ferns.) From the ford return the way you came, past your descending path. Ford a shallow stream and walk ahead to a wide track. On your right now are the scant remains of a ROMAN AQUEDUCT, where a waterfall disgorges into a lovely pool.

Follow the track (RED WAYMARKS) uphill through pine and oak, with white cliffs all around you. You come to two METAL POSTS (1h), where a faint path goes left towards a rock wall. Ignore this but, just beyond it, turn left on a good strong path (GREEN WAY-MARKS). *(The Alternative walks continue straight ahead here, along the track.)*

There are paths all along here, so keep ahead (northwest) on the main path, weaving through limestone boulders. As you double back above your outgoing route, you can see it below on the left, in a small valley swamped with pines. After 10 minutes you join the main track to the dam: bear left downhill. After just a

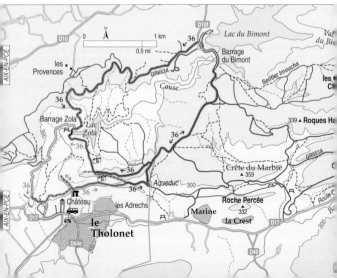

Just a tiny reservoir; nothing special, you might think; but this dam, while only 42m high and 68m long, is in all the engineering textbooks.

couple of minutes there is a beautiful view of the jade-green lake from some rocks off to the right. The Croix de Provence rises on the right, challenging you to try Walk 35.

When you reach **Lac Zola** (**1h25min**), cross the DAM. It was built in the mid-19th century by the father of Emile Zola (see page 65) and was one of the first arch dams in the world. The rock ledges here are good picnic spots.

Take the metalled lane leading uphill from the dam, passing the old KEEPER'S HOUSE on the right (now run by the Office National des Forêts). Soon a wide track curves in front of you in a big U-bend (**1h45min**); this leads to Bibemus, where Cézanne used to paint. Don't curve uphill to Bibemus, go left downhill on the lane. Some 15 minutes later you pass the knoll at the start of the walk and continue back to the CHATEAU in **Le Tholonet** (**2h10min**).

TRAIN DES PIGNES

Departures: from Nice daily at 6.55, 09.25, 13.05, 17.15; from Digne at 07.15, 10.45, 14.25, 17.35. *Journey time 3h 25min.* There are other departures north and south from Annot: see www.train provence.com/english for timetables and prices. The same operators, Chemins de Fer de Provence, also run a touristic steam train between Puget-Théniers and Annot. *Hints:* The little train is very comfortable, with 'sightseeing-size' windows. Travelling south, sit on the left; travelling north, sit on the right. *Don't make the mistake of sitting in the front row* — the ticket collector monopolises the front windows! Take a map, to pinpoint all the sights en route. The train stops for a good five minutes at Annot, where those 'in the know' take a break at the pleasant station restaurant. *Be warned:* If you are based in Nice, you won't even have time for a long lunch in Digne unless you take the first train of the day. But it's a very relaxing way of sightseeing — so we just pack a picnic…

No trip to the south of France is complete without a journey on the delightful Train des Pignes (perhaps named for the pine cones the locals collected on Sundays to take back home). After the County of Nice was returned to France in 1860, there was great interest in linking the newly re-won Alps (see photo caption page 107) with the coast. Every valley wanted its own train. One of the surprisingly numerous projects to get off the drawing board, despite obstacles of terrain and financing, was the line built from Nice to Digne between 1890 and 1912 — spanning 150km via 16 viaducts, 17 bridges, and 25 tunnels, one of them 3km long! Some other railways built at this time, at enormous cost and effort, have not survived: the viaducts on the line to Barcelonnette are now drowned beneath the Lac de Serre-Ponçon; the Caramel Viaduct passed on Car tour 2 is the sad remains of the route from Menton to Sospel.

The train is not only worth taking for the sightseeing, but an extremely pleasant way to get to walks (Walks 25 and 26 lie en route). It's a 'friendly' train, too, and will stop to drop off or pick up walkers virtually anywhere along the run. At all the stations or on their website (see above) you should be able to find or download a brochure with five other walks from the train — only available in French. Please bear in mind that the walks vary enormously in interest and difficulty and *should not be attempted without the relevant large-scale IGN map!*
Leaving Nice, the train moves like a tram through the city and into the suburbs. Soon it's hurtling along the wide basin of the *Var*. At **Colomars** look up left, above the industrial spread of modern-day Carros beside the Var, to *Carros-Village* and *Le Broc* perched on

168

Trains at Annot, one of them prepared for a snowfall. These are the old-style trains: on their website you'll see the streamlined new cars

the hillside. At **St-Martin-du-Var**, the *Esteron Valley* comes in from the left. Beyond **Plan-du-Var**, don't miss the mouth of the *Vésubie Gorge*, seen through the Pont Durandy on the right. The perched village of *Bonson* rises on the left. Now you're in the *Defilé du Chaudan*, between the two carriageways of the D6202, racing the motorists. Utelle cannot be seen above the olive terraces, but *do* look out right (just beyond a tunnel) for the towering walls of the *Tinée Gorge*, backed by the *Mercantour*. Colourful small-holdings introduce **Toüet-sur-Var**, huddled below a rock cliff. Then the most magnificent of all the gorges opens up — the *Cians Gorge*. Look up to the rock blades behind **Puget-**

Théniers: Alternative walk 25 scales those cliffs. A 5km-long stretch of orchards and plane trees lines the way from here to **Entrevaux**, the fairy-tale village shown on page 41. Past the gap of the *Daluis Gorge*, watch for some high bluffs on the right: Walk 26 rounds a ledge almost at the very top. At **Annot** notice the houses built into boulders like those shown in the photograph on page 138 *(Grès d'Annot)* and the chaos of *grès* just as you leave, as well as the *robines* (see page 173). Now the train hurtles through the rolling fields and orchards of the verdant *Vaire Valley* to **Méailles**. A 3km-long tunnel precedes **Thorame-Haute-Gare**. Still the little train tears along, shrugging off the fact that it has already climbed 1000m from Nice! The gorgeous *Verdon Valley* is followed to **St-André**. You have a fine view of the church and the *Lac de Castillon* as you leave: watch for paragliders

169

here. Following the *Asse de Moriez*, come to **Moriez**: just outside it there are interesting rock dykes. A 12th-century chapel rises on a hill outside **Barrême**, where a huge fir graces the station. Now the N85 *(Route Napoléon)* is just beside you on the right, and you skirt the *Forêt Domaniale des Trois Asses,* as you follow the Asse de Blieux via the *Clue de Chabrières* (on the left) to **Châteauredon**. From here the train curves north and crosses the wide *Bléone,* before coming into **Digne** (*i✝M♩♫*), below the Alpes de Haute-Provence. Out of the station, turn left to walk into town (15 minutes).

Vauban's gate at Entrevaux

Glossary

Baume: cave, shelter beneath rock

Belvédère: elevated viewpoint

Bergerie: shelter for animals (and sometimes shepherds)

Borie: drystone dwelling. Bories are thought to date from the Bronze Age (while their exact origin is unknown, they resemble drystone dwellings as far afield as Ireland, Sardinia, the Balearics and Peru). There are not very many in eastern Provence, but a fine example is on the Plateau de Calern near Claps (Car tour 3, photograph overleaf).

Buvette: snack bar

CAF: Club Alpin Français

Calanque: rocky inlet

Castelas, castellas, castellaras: old ruined castle; see Walk 18.

Chasse privée: private hunting ground

Cime: summit, peak, top

Cirque: a valley ending in a deep rounded 'amphitheatre' of rock (photographs pages 8-9, 106-107, 114)

Clos: enclosed parcel of cultivated land

Clue: narrow gorge or rift, cut by a watercourse perpendicularly to a chain of mountains; see Car tours 6 and 7 and photographs on page 140 and right

Col: pass

Dégustation: wine-tasting

Dolomitic rock: rock composed of soluble calcium and less soluble magnesium. The calcium erodes more quickly under the action of rainwater and streams, giving rise to weird formations, for which the French have a very apt name (*ruiniform*).

Domaine: property (vineyard; see photograph page 64)

Dyke: basaltic magma injected into a fissure in rocks, sometimes weathered into a wall-like form

Garrigue, Maquis: terrain resulting from the degradation of the Mediterranean forest (through fires or grazing), differentiated by the nature of their soil and characteristic flora. The *garrigue* is an open limestone wasteland on non-acidic soil, with small pockets of vegetation. Typical plants include Aleppo pines, kermes oak, holm oak, box, thistles, gorse, rough grass and wild aromatic plants like lavender, thyme and rosemary. The

Clue de St-Auban: unlike the other clues on Car tour 7, you can drive through this one on a good, amply-wide road.

Large borie *on the Plateau de Calern, near Les Claps (Car tour 3); some bories have been converted into 'bijou' holiday homes.*

maquis is a dense covering of evergreen plants growing on acidic soil, usually with small hairy or leathery leaves to help withstand the dry conditions. Flora include trees like cork and holm oaks, junipers, box, strawberry trees (see photograph opposite) and myrtle, as well as smaller bushes like rosemary, Jerusalem sage, broom, heather, and *Cistus*. Larger trees like chestnuts and maritime pines may also be present.

Gouffre: gulf, abyss

GR (Grande Randonnée): long-distance footpath, way-marked with red and white paint flashes; see page 73.

Grès: sand- or gritstone, eroded into strange shapes. A chaos of gigantic sandstone rocks and arches is the most prominent feature of the landscape around Annot; photographs pages 138, 139 (Walk 26).

Grotte: cave

Maquis: see Garrigue

Maquis, The: French Resistance during World War II

Mas: country house, usually applied to a farm

Massif: mountain mass with several peaks

Oppidum: defensive position of dry-stone walls at vantage points. The Ligurians built the first *oppida*. See Walk 18.

PR (Petite Randonnée): local waymarked walk, fairly short, often circular; see page 73.

Porphyry rock: hard rock in which crystals of one or more minerals are deposited; the colour depends on the metallic content. Red porphyry rock characterises the Esterel (Car tour 1 and Walks 5-7), but you will also find small examples of blue or green porphyry rock.

Rive droite, rive gauche: right bank, left bank of a river. (The banks of a river are defined *from* the source.)

Robines (roubines): limey-clay slopes prone to erosion. They form steep and slippery gulleys — difficult (and potentially dangerous) walking terrain. Prevalent in Haute-Provence, they are the

Right: robines *near the Crête d'Aurafort (Alternative walk 25);* below: *the strawberry tree is a familiar sight in the* maquis.

most obvious feature of the landscape around St-André (Car tour 5); photographs on pages 51, 143 and right.

Roche, Rocher: rock

Route Napoléon: The old, iconic *route nationale* N85, opened in 1932 (and recently renumbered by the *départements* through which it runs). See Car tour 4 and photographs on pages 29, 30, 125.

Ruiniform: a word the French use to describe a chaos of dolomitic rock, which has eroded into the shape of ruins. They may look like a building or even a whole town, or sometimes a ruined sculpture. The Cadières de Brandis, shown on pages 6-7, are an example of *ruiniform* dolomitic rock.

Sentier (botanique): footpath. (A *sentier botanique* is usually accompanied by information panels describing the botany and geology of a specific area; there is a particularly interesting *sentier botanique* at the Lac d'Allos, Walk 23.)

Table d'orientation: panoramic viewpoint, usually with a circular stone 'table' marked with the points of the compass and pin-pointing the location of towns, mountains, etc.

Transhumance: periodic migration of sheep, in order to graze on the high mountains in summer and return to the lower slopes in the autumn. This movement of flocks has been carried out by lorry in modern times, but in the last few years some shepherds have returned to the ancient

practice of making the journey with their flocks on foot.

Via: road. By 100BC Rome held much of the land between the Alps and the Pyrenees. Their most important highways were the *Via Agrippa* via Orange and Avignon to Arles, the *Via Aurelia* via Nice, Fréjus, Aix and Nîmes to Arles and then Spain (today the M6007/D6007/DN7 follows much the same route), and the *Via Domitia* via Sisteron, Apt and Pont Julien south to the *Via Aurelia*.

Restaurants

We only feature below places we visit regularly (including some of our favourite hotel stops on the car tours). *All* of these restaurants specialise in regional dishes, and all have decent wine lists. Since we often have the house wine, we've not gone into details of the wines. Prices range from € (inexpensive) to €€€ (fairly pricey) — don't be surprised to see €-€€€; you can have a relatively inexpensive meal in a top-class establishment if you choose just one course a la carte, the dish of the day, or the weekday *formule* — with 250 ml house wine.

Aix-en-Provence

LA ROTONDE €-€€€
2A, Place Jeanne d'Arc (facing the Fontaine de la Rotonde at the start of the Cours Mirabeau), daily all year, 08.00-02.00; ☎ 04 42 91 61 70; www.larotonde-aix.com. No need to go into great detail here: their website tells you everything you want to know about ambience and food (although it is only in French at present). All we need say is: the location is marvellous, the staff extremely helpful and the dishes we had at last visit (risotto with gambas, foie gras sautéed with apples and port sauce) superb.

LE PIGONNET €€€
5 Avenue du Pigonnet, open all year, 12.00-13.45 and 19.00-21.30; ☎ 04 42 59 02 90, www.hotelpigonnet.com. A 10-15 minute walk from the centre, this gorgeous **estate hotel** is set in beautiful, peaceful gardens looking out to where Cézanne painted Ste-Victoire. Elegant and comfortable public spaces and rooms, superb food and wine (see their website). Very pricey, even the Mon-Fri luncheon *menu* (3 courses) is 35 €. But it's just heaven — a place to treat yourself, if only for one night!

Aspremont

HOSTELLERIE D'ASPREMONT €-€€
Place St-Claude; ☎ 04 93 08 00 05, www.hostellerie-aspremont.com. Walkers are assured a very friendly welcome in this small, homely hotel. The building was once a farm and is one of the oldest in the village. There's an open fire in the dining room in winter; in summer you'll want to eat out on the terrace with its fine views. **Three** *menus* are usually offered, all the same price and all include cheese and sweet. The emphasis is on local food and wines. Should the restaurant be closed, Chez Mireille opposite also has fine views — and crispy-base pizzas!

Beuil

There are several restaurants in Beuil. Closing dates are erratic; they open for the summer walking season and again for the winter skiing season, closing in spring and autumn. We particularly like the **HOTEL L'ESCAPADE** €-€€, on the main road to the church, open every day all year round; restaurant open 12.00-14.00 and 19.30-21.00; *menu* at 25 € (☎ 04 93 02 31 27, www.hrlescapade.fr). Very friendly staff, regional cooking, pretty terrace. You can see their menus on the website (under the search icon, key in 'menu'). We usually eat here a la carte, because the 'entrée' on the menu is a meal in itself. It's a beautifully presented *assiette terroir,* which you serve yourself from platters brought to the table — *terrine de foie de volaille* (chicken liver and mushroom), sliced headcheese (brawn) and cured ham, various pickles and huge jars of wild *sanguin* mushrooms in olive oil. The **fish** course features **local trout** in basil sauce; **meats** include steaks, *daube de boeuf*, tripe sausage *(andouillette)*. For a lighter meal, there's a wide range of **pastas** and *petits farcis* (described below under Nice, René Socca).

Cannes
LA MERE BESSON €€
13 Rue des Frères Pradignac, cl Sun from Sep-Jun, open for *dinner only; menus* at 31 €, 48 €; ℂ 04 93 39 59 24, no website. This restaurant opened in the 1930s and quickly became famous for authentic Provençal cooking — an 'in' place, especially during the Film Festival. Although 'Mother' Besson is long dead, her devotees return year after year to enjoy some of the dishes that made the restaurant famous — like creamy **chicken with tarragon**, *estouffade* (braised beef in red wine with onions and mushrooms), *bourride* (fish stew), **shoulder of lamb** with Provençal herbs and garlic purée. There are different **main-course specials** every day; Fridays are popular for the *aïoli* — a stew of desalted dried cod, vegetables and a creamy garlic *aïoli* sauce. *Be sure to reserve in advance!*

Eze
LE NID D'AIGLE €€
1 Rue du Château, open daily from 09.00-21.30; ℂ 04 93 41 19 08, www.leniddaigle-eze.com. There are restaurants galore in Eze. Unless you just want an ice-cream, give the ones near the main road a miss and walk up to the very top of the village. Here you'll find the *very welcoming* Nid d'Aigle, a homely place with stone and wood décor, Provençal fabrics on the tables, and fantastic views over the village rooftops to the sea. In fine weather you can eat out on the walled terrace, under the shade of a venerable mulberry tree. The same family have run the place for 20 years. Even in winter there is a wide range of **drinks, sweets, breakfasts till 11.30, snacks all day**; nine **entrées** — salads, *escargots*, charcuterie; three kinds of **fish**, depending on the season; **meat**: pork, steak and beef tartare; **tagliatellis** with different sauces. The food is beautifully prepared, subtly flavoured, and simply delicious. On their website you can see a slideshow of 25 of their dishes.

Lac de St-Cassien
LES ARBOUSIERS €-€€
At Lac de St-Cassien, closed Mon throughout the year, also 20 Nov-15 Dec. Open May-Oct 12.00-15.30 and 19.00-21.00, in low season only open for lunch; ℂ 04 93 60 67 89; no website. Often we just spend a week or more in Nice, checking tours and walks from there. It was very convenient to take Exit 39 (Fayence) off the A8 motorway and have a coffee or tea at Les Arbousiers, just above the lake. We stopped so often that the owner wanted to sell us the place when he retired. Eventually he *did* sell to a Brit, and our only disappointment is that there is no more morning coffee or afternoon tea — just set meal times. The Friday **fish and chips special** is going down a treat with the locals as well as the expats. But the new owner is a keen chef: some of his dishes can be seen on Trip Advisor. The setting, inside or on the terrace overlooking the lake, is delightful. There is also a beach and pedalo rental.

Menton
There are two choices here, depending on time and budget.
HOTEL LE TERMINUS €, by the railway station, is open daily from 07.00-23.00. This friendly,

family-run place has a cheerful atmosphere and is ideal for those in a hurry. It's very conveniently located, specialises in regional dishes and is amazingly cheap.

LE BRUIT QUI COURT €€-€€€

31 Quai Bonaparte, open Wed-Sun for lunch and dinner; (04 93 35 94 64; www.lebruitqui court.fr. This lovely restaurant at the port is ideal for a relaxing meal. Unlike many other places, their *menu* (24 €) offers *three* courses, and there is a a choice from six **entrées** — like scrambled eggs and smoked salmon or baked stuffed crab; six **mains** — seafood, fish, meat or vegetarian; **dessert** of the day. **Specialities** include **risotto** with scampi and saffron and **grills** like tuna with duck foie gras. There is also a **gourmet** *menu* at 39 €: three courses from anything on the imaginative menu — perhaps starting with foie gras and confit of Corsican cherries or lobster in champagne sauce with almonds. People rave about their lemon tart. Of course, where better than Menton to have it!

Nice

Since Nice is usually our base, we have a wider selection here.

RENÉ SOCCA €

2 Rue Mirhaletti, daily ex Mon from 09.00-21.00; (04 93 92 05 73. If you want to try *socca*, Nice's speciality dish, it's best to go to Old Nice, where it's widely available. Our favourite place is René's — a *very busy* open-fronted shop on the corner of Rue Pairolière and Rue Mirhaletti, surrounded by thick wooden tables and benches. Of course in Nice it's usually pleasant to eat outdoors, but if it's too sunny, too cold or raining, there is also *indoor seating* (most first-timers don't realise this); the entrance is opposite the *socca* window. René's sells far more than *socca*, and here's our second tip. The

socca is sold from a window on Rue Mirhaletti; all the other food is sold from Rue Pairolière. There are two queues, and the *socca* queue is by far the longer — it stretches round the block into Rue Pairolière, so you have to try to find where it ends! Keep approaching *local* people with the word '*socca*'; if they nod, they should be in the *socca* queue... So the strategy is this: one person queues for the food, while the others find a table and order the drinks (it is compulsory to buy something to drink if you are sitting at any table, indoors or out). If you are *only* having *socca*, make for the *socca* queue. Admittedly, the dozens of dishes stacked up in the main window look cold and rather unappealing, but as soon as you have chosen (just point to what you want), they heat it up for you. By this time you should have moved round to the *socca* window, and the piping-hot *socca* should be served in a trice, as it's coming out of the fires every few minutes. *Petits farcis* and *fritures* go especially well with *socca*. And rosé wine (by the glass) is the preferred drink of the locals, although there is also Normandy cider and beer. Selections from the menu include: *socca* (chick-pea 'pancake', eaten with the fingers); *petits farcis* (stuffed courgettes, onions, peppers); **pizza**; **pissaladière** (a pizza with onion, black olives and anchovies); deep-fried **courgette flowers**; **aubergine** and **courgette** fritters; **cabillaud** (spicy fritters made from dried cod — Fridays only); **fritures** (whitebait); **sardines** and lemon; *daube* (beef stew) with polenta; *pan bagnat* (thick sandwich; the bread is moistened with olive oil and vinegar); *tourte de blettes* (chard pie); **sweet *tartes***.

BALTHAZAR €-€€

3 Promenade des Anglais, daily from 08.00-01.00 (11.00 in

winter); (04 91 16 53 64. We first found this place when we were staying up in the wilds of Puget-Théniers (see Walk 25) in cold, rainy weather. We took the Train des Pignes to Nice and just headed for the sea! The nearest bright lights shone at a café on the corner of Halévy and the Promenade, just a few doors east of the tourist office. It's now under new ownership and called Balthazar and even better than it was. Of course, the setting looking out to sea is perfect, and plenty of seating outside lets you make the most of it. Although it's not a 'restaurant' proper, there's plenty of choice for a full meal. Balthazar is not inexpensive, but the food is scrumptious. A great place to have **English breakfast** — or continental — from 08.00 till noon; **soups**, **sandwiches**, **burgers**, **pizzas**; **omelettes** and **salads** — like niçoise and beautifully fresh cobb; enticing **meat and fish platters** — tapas, Italian hams, foie gras, chicken wings, smoked salmon, carpaccio of beef, beef tartare. There are also savoury and sweet **crêpes**, grilled **steaks** and **duck**, with frites; and for just a snack, **ice-creams**, a **sweet trolley** and a wide array of **teas** and **cocktails**.

CAFE DE TURIN €-€€€
5 Place Garibaldi, daily all year from 08.00-23.00; (04 93 62 29 52, www.cafedeturin.com. *The* place in Nice for **fish** — particularly **shellfish** — everything from the popular sea bass to 10 varieties of oyster, and sea urchins in season. An institution; always full, ensuring the freshest of food. The **huge menu** features dozens of different **fish** dishes prepared to order — grilled, baked, poached, sauced. Or try their **seafood platters** (two are shown on the website). For those who don't fancy seafood there are meat dishes and even pizza and *socca*.

TAVERNE MASSENA €€
25 Rue Masséna, daily non-stop; (04 93 87 77 57, www.crescere. fr. This is one of three restaurants in the Cresci chain, all in the heart of the pedestrian zone. Work up an appetite in advance by checking out their full menus online — it's likely they'll have whatever you fancy eating! The food is exceptionally good. On our last visit we loved the aubergine *au gratin* and the (very light) beef tartare. There's a **Sunday brunch special** at 34 € *including drinks.* **Specialities** include dishes from Alsace, with several choucroutes. Their *assiette provençale* is a good introduction to several regional specialities: it features *pissaladière* (Provençal 'pizza', topped with caramelised onions and black olives), a tomato stuffed with seasoned mince, *panisses* (chick pea 'cakes'), battered cod *(morue)*, tomato dipping sauce, a tiny but perfect in its freshness *salade niçoise*, battered and plain aubergines.

CHEZ FREDDY €€
22 Cours Saleya, daily from 11.00 to 23.30 non stop; (04 93 85 49 99, www.chezfreddy.com. Set right smack in the middle of Cours Saleya, where there are dozens and dozens of restaurants. But even in the middle of a torrential downpour we're fussy: we chose it because it has a lovely view to the Palais de Justice *and* the waterfall on the Colline du Château — both illuminated at night. It wasn't till we got home that we read it's recommended by Trip Advisor and Michelin.

Beware the moules *at Chez Freddy as a starter: there must have been over 100 mussels in this serving…*

Oysters at the Café de Turin, a landmark on Place Garibaldi in Nice

best sampled at leisure. Yes, it's pricey, but the food is divine (see photos on their website). If your budget doesn't stretch to the main restaurant — or you're in walking boots, why not stop on the terrace for a hot or cold drink? The staff are most welcoming. The **luncheon** *menu* at 32 € *(not available on Sun/holidays)* includes a main course, dessert, and glass of wine). The main **evening** *menus* (52 €, 62 €) usually feature eight different **entrées** — like broad bean soup with savoury, new onions, fresh cows' cheese and lightly grilled mountain ham; nine **main courses**, ranging from **fish** (fried fillets of red mullet with a compote of tomatoes, tiny purple artichokes and the juice of Menton lemons) to **poultry** (roasted farm-raised guinea fowl on a polenta base, with fig and cherry sauce) to **meat** (milk-fed lamb cooked in the traditional way); a small but intriguing **cheese board**; eight different **desserts** — like nougat ice cream with honey and grilled caramelized almonds.

The huge menu, with dozens of mouth-watering photos (and some recipes!), can be seen and downloaded before you travel. There is an **evening** *menu* at 25,90 €. Chez Freddy specialises in fish and seafood, with a huge choice of dishes — 6 different aïolis (fish stews), 6 types of paella, 6 sorts of bouillabaisse. Also 10 starters, 8 mains (not only dishes like skate in white wine sauce, but meats like rib-eye beef), 10 sweets. There are pastas and pizzas, even sushis(!)

Peillon
AUBERGE DE LA MADONE €€€
Place Auguste-Arnulf, cl Wed, 9 Nov-31 Jan (except for Christmas holidays); (04 93 79 91 17, www.auberge-madone-peillon. com/en. This family-run hotel and restaurant is praised in all the up-market guides. Father and son do the cooking; vegetables and herbs come from their own garden. This is fine cuisine and

Puget-Théniers
L'OUSTALET €-€€
At the railway station, 09.00 until last dinner is served; cl Sun after 3pm; (04 93 05 04 11; *menus* at 14 €, 20 €, 23 €; **gourmet** *menu* 27 €). This restaurant might go unnoticed if you make straight for Puget centre (it's housed in the old station *buffet*). *Don't* miss it! It's a *very* popular, excellent place, run by a husband/wife team specialising in local dishes. It's very cosy in winter, but in fine weather we like to watch the comings and goings of the Train de Pignes or the steam train, so we sit beside the railway line, out on the Virginia creeper-covered terrace. There is a huge, quite sophisticated selection, from **light meals** (sandwiches,

omelettes, *secca* (an Entrevaux speciality: dried salt beef with olive oil and lemon juice), and 8 kinds of *bruschetta;* **fresh pastas** (with 10 different sauces); **fish** including locally-caught trout, sea bass, sole; **meat** from duck to veal, sweetbreads, goulash of wild boar, *daube*, steaks with varied sauces. We're quite thrilled to read all the excellent reviews about L'Oustalet on Trip Advisor and other sites because we think we were the first to 'discover' this place and publicise it to an English-speaking audience!

Rians

HOSTELLERIE DE L'ESPLANADE €€
Place du Colombier, open 11.45-13.30 and 19.00-21.00; cl Wed/Sun evenings and from 22/12 to 26/1; ☏ 04 94 80 31 12; weekday *formule* lunch 13.50 € (15.00 € Sat/Sun), **dinner** 28.00 €; *menu terroir* 24.00 €; *menu gourmand* 34.00 €. Very traditional, old-fashioned hotel and restaurant, with very friendly service (family-owned).A good lunch stop. 8 **entrées**, including really **superb salads** like farm salad with *chevre* and ham, *salade gourmande* with foie gras and gambas. 2 **fish** dishes (depending on catch), also gambas and scallops. The **meat** mains are a bit boring — the standard steak, pork, lamb; **sweet** trolley.

St-Jean-Cap-Ferrat

There are dozens of restaurants in Cap Ferrat and nearby Beaulieu, ranging from 5-star to smaller bistros, *créperies* and ice cream parlours. Many of the restaurants beside the port at St-Jean are open all year round and, if the day is fine, this is where everyone congregates to enjoy the lively atmosphere. If you want to dine with the stars, then *the* place to be seen is
LE SLOOP €€-€€€
At the harbour; ☏ 04 93 01 48

63; cl Wed in winter and 15/11-20/12. A beautifully decorated *restaurant gastronomique*, but with a lunch *menu* at about 33 €. Another popular place, *not* on the harbour, is

CAPITAINE COOK €€-€€€
11 Avenue Jean-Mermoz, open 12.30-14.30 and 19.30-22.30; cl all day Wed, Thu lunch, and 8/11-26/12; ☏ 04 93 76 02 66. A long-standing seafood restaurant with a very pretty vine-covered terrace and cosy interior. Rumour has it that it was the inspiration for the film *Casablanca* — in the 1930s it had a pianist called Sam. *Menu* at 27 €; à la carte 35 €-55 €. The **speciality** is all kinds of **seafood**, prepared in a myriad of ways, but there are **poultry** and **meat dishes**, like half chicken with mushrooms in a cream sauce, slivered calves liver with shallots, guinea fowl *(pintadeau)*, lamb fricassee, and various steaks.

St-Martin Vésubie

Two hotels/restaurants here.

LA BONNE AUBERGE €€
on the main M2565 in the centre of St-Martin (cl 15/11-1/2; ☏ 04 93 03 20 49, www.labonne auberge06.fr). This family-run (since 1946) hotel and restaurant offers simple rooms and a cosily cluttered cellar restaurant with a large open fire. There's also a very pretty terrace for fine-weather dining. The 3-course *menus* at 25 € and 31 € both feature hearty portions of regional specialities, and there is plenty of choice.

LE BOREON €€ is another hotel just beside the lake at Le Boréon in the Mercantour National Park (cl 1/11-10/1; ☏ 04 93 03 20 35, www.hotel-boreon.com). Pretty, bright dining room and lovely terrace overlooking the lake. The setting is of course magical. We have not stayed there, only stopped for tea.

Théoule-sur-Mer
MARCO POLO €€
47 Avenue des Lérins, cl Mon in winter and 13/11-18/12; otherwise open 09.30-00.30; (04 93 49 96 59; www.marcopolo-beach.com. *Menu* at 32 € (having just one à la carte dish is far less pricey). **Fish** is the speciality (try the mixed seafood grill, served with a lovely mayonnaise sauce), but there is **meat** as well, from duck to kid *(chevreau)* to steaks; morning **coffee**, afternoon **tea**, **snacks** and drinks all day. Rooftop tapas bar in summer. A most relaxed atmosphere, right on the sea, with an outdoor terrace. Run by the same family over three generations.

Turbie, La
LE CAFÉ DE LA FONTAINE €-€€
4 Avenue du Général de Gaulle, daily 07.00-24.00, cl Mon in winter; (04 93 28 52 79. Go to www.hostelleriejerome.com, then click on 'le café de la fontaine' — to see what a superb lunch or dinner you could have for just 25 €! The menu changes daily, depending on what's in the market. And you won't feel out of place in walking gear, despite the fact that it's owned by the very swish and expensive Hostellerie Jérôme (with two Michelin stars).

Turini, Col de
LES TROIS VALLEES €-€€
Col de Turini, open all year; (04 93 04 23 23, www.les3vallees-turini.fr; 2 *menus* at 28 € and 33 €. The Col de Turini comes alive with the Monte Carlo Rally in January (when it must be deafening), but in early spring and autumn, when the area is at its best for walking, all is silence. So it's a wonderful place to spend the night. At least stop for afternoon tea on their terrace — especially in September, when the rowans are weighed down with fat red berries. **Specialities** include **entrées** like salad with mountain ham, *sanguin* mushrooms, crêpes filled with goats' cheese and minced mushrooms; **mains:** venison stew, trout stuffed with *foie gras* and apples in Normandy sauce, veal fillet with *girolles* (wild mushrooms); **desserts:** myrtle or raspberry tarte, *crème brûlée* with lavender.

Verdon, Grand Canyon du
Our very favourite place to stay here is the top-class, medieval **CHATEAU DE TRIGANCE** €€-€€€ in the eponymous village ((04 94 76 91 18, www.chateau-de-trigance.fr), shown on page 53. Ask for room 1! There is a history and some panoramic views on their website — including the romantic vaulted dining room. Top-class food (menus on their website). Far less sophisticated/expensive is the **AUBERGE DU POINT SUBLIME** €-€€ on the D952 above the Samson Corridor ((04 92 83 60 35, www.auberge-pointsublime.com). Simple rooms and plain cooking of local specialities; breakfasts with delicious **thick local honey**. *Menus* at 18 €, 27 €, 31.50 € and (gourmand) 37.50 €. Both here and at Trigance, autumn mornings are utterly exhilarating, as the mist clears from the mountaintops.

Vésubie, Gorges de la
On the M2565 there's a pleasant morning coffee/afternoon tea stop: the **AUBERGE DU BON PUITS** at Le Suquet (between Lantosque and St-Jean-la-Rivière). The cosy bar/café at the front of the hotel is ideal in winter for a bracing hot chocolate, the shady outdoor terrace in hot weather for a cooling drink. Pleasant staff; there are local goodies and even books for sale. No doubt you could get a good meal here too.

☀ Index

Geographical names comprises the only entries in this Index; for all other entries, see Contents, page 3. A page number in *italics* indicates a map; a page number in **bold** a photograph. Both of these may be in addition to a text reference on the same page. Recommended restaurants are shown by the symbol ✕; market days by the symbol ৬৯.

181